**The Gregg Method**

**of Fire Control**

*Branded for my very good friend Roy Shogren*
*6-25-09*
*Jim Gregg*

# The Gregg Method of Fire Control

A Training Manual
on Point Shooting
Handguns and Shotguns

## James B. Gregg

Edited by Gordon Schneider and Tina Talbot

COPYRIGHT © 2004
by Jim Gregg's Shooting Schools, Inc.
P.O. Box 1158
Moses Lake, Washington 98837

First Edition, October 2004

Published by
Jim Gregg's Shooting Schools, Inc.

Email: www.gunguyjimgregg@yahoo.com
Website: www.JimGregg.net

All rights reserved. No part of this book may be used or reproduced in any manner whatsoever without written permission except in the case of brief quotations found in the contents of this book.

Book design by Kathryn E. Campbell,
Gorham Printing, Rochester, Washington

For information, address:
Jim Gregg's Shooting Schools, Inc.
P.O. Box 1158
Moses Lake, WA 98837

Library of Congress Catalog No. 2004096642

Softcover ISBN 0-9759068-0-1
Hardcover ISBN 0-9759068-1-X

Photographs by Jim Gregg's Shooting Schools
unless otherwise noted.

Printed in the U.S.A.

# Dedication

To the men and women who enforce the law.

My reason for training law enforcement for the past 30 years is simply because the officer has the highest probability of weapon use.

Skillful point-shooting can be a very accurate method of shooting handguns and shotguns under conditions that exist most of the time in deadly confrontations.

I feel that traditional methods of firearms training are only a beginning in learning the ultimate use of handguns and shotguns under combat conditions.

—Jim Gregg

# Preface

I write this book with the hope that its contents will help those in law enforcement survive a deadly confrontation. I have never believed that when caught in a situation in which deadly force is necessary an officer will use target shooting methods of handgun shooting and take his eyes off an armed criminal to focus the front sight on the handgun. It's like driving a car by looking at the hood ornament; it's not a natural sequence in firing the handgun in a combat situation.

Skillful Point-Shooting is the most natural way of shooting handguns and shotguns in close-quarter situations.

# Acknowledgments

My first acknowledgement goes to my wife Delores who has prodded me for the past several years to put my life story into writing for the handgun and shotgun shooter. Delores has supported me in typing the manuscript and struggling with the complications of putting it all into our computer when neither of us knows much about computers. *Thank you Delores.*

Special thanks to Dave Smith of Elma, Washington, a student of the martial arts, for providing information on "Arjuna the Archer".

Special thanks to the following Border Patrol Agents (active and retired) who have supported me and the contents of this book with pictures of drug apprehensions and real life stories involving drug activity, shooting incidents and statistics on the extent of illegal drug activity out of just a single Border Patrol Station.

GORDON SCHNEIDER, P.A.I.C., Eagle Pass, Texas, Retired
"The Gordon Schneider Incident"
"The Azrack-Newton Abduction and BPA Murder"
"Loma Linda Ranch Episode"
"Bob Gilbert Shooting"

JERRELL EDMISON, Retired
" Maurice Dixon & Warren O'Neal Incident"
"A Tale of the Tiger"

BILL GLENN, Retired
"East Desert Shootout"

DAVID TOOTHMAN
S.R.T. Leader, Del Rio, Texas
"Shooting Incident, Vega Verde Area"

ALAN GORDON, Retired
"Alan Gordon Shooting Incident"
"Jewel Valley Shootout"

## Contents

Preface / 7

Acknowledgments / 9

Foreword / 15

Early Experiences with Firearms / 23

   Developing the Gregg Method of Fire Control / 26

   Seattle Gun Club / 26

Teaching Point-Shooting the Shotgun / 29

   Eliminating the Air Rifle as a Step between the Shooter and the Target / 30

   Learning to Point-Shoot the Shotgun / 32

      Monkey See–Monkey Do! / 34

Your Eye System and How It Relates to Accurate Shotgun Shooting / 35

      Physical or Psychological Errors / 37

### The Basics in Handling the Shotgun / 38

   The Carry Position / 39

   The Ready Position / 44

   The Forearm / 45

   The Grip / 45

   The Side of the Body / 47

   The Final Position / 48

   Mounting the Shotgun to the Face / 49

   Chinning the Stock / 51

   Female Shooters / 52

   Taller Than Average Shooters / 54

Fitting the Shooter to the Shotgun / 56

Fixing a Shotgun to Fit Perfectly / 57

Correcting the Most Common Shotgun Shooting Problems / 59

   Peeking / 59

   A Right-Handed Shooter Shooting to the Left with Both Eyes Open / 59

   Left-Handed Shotgun Shooter Shooting to the Right with Both Eyes Open / 60

   Right- or Left-Handed Shooters Shooting High on Straight-Away Targets / 60

   Open Sighted Shotguns / 60

   Peep-Sighted Shotguns / 61

Range Activity (Two Day Shooting School) / 62

   Target Holders / 62

   Training with Clay Targets / 63

   Point-Shooting the Shotgun after a Pursuit / 68

   Learning to Lead a Target / 70

      How Not To Lead a Target / 72

   Daytime Shooting-Single Targets with Buckshot / 73

   Nighttime Shooting with a Plain-Barreled Shotgun with a Tritium Pointer (Bead) / 73

   Nighttime shooting with sighted shot guns with a standard stock / 74

   Multiple Targets at Nighttime / 74

Maintaining a Level of Proficiency by Visualization / 74

The Mind's Eye—The Eye of The Subconscious / 75

**A Training Manual on Point Shooting Handguns / 77**

Beginning to be a Point-Shooter with the Handgun / 79

The Eye System / 83

Eye Combinations / 84

Master Eye / 85

   1. Right Master Eye / 85

   2. Eyes Balanced / 86

   3. Right Handed/Left Master Eye / 88

   4. Right Handed/Right Dominant Eye / 93

   5. Right Handed/Left Dominant Eye / 94

   6. Left Handed/Left Master Eye / 95

   7. Right Handed/Right Master Eye (Unstable) / 96

   8. Left Handed 50/50 Vision / 96

   9. Left Handed/Right Master Eye / 97

   10. Left Handed/Left Dominant Eye / 98

   11. Left Handed/Right Dominant Eye / 99

   12. Right Handed/Left Master Eye (Unstable) / 100

   13. Double Cross Dominant / 100

   14. Parallel Dominant / 101

   Another Exotic Eye Combination / 102

Checking the Eye System / 103

Problems in Shooting Straight / 104

   Shooting High / 104

   Shooting Low / 104

   Shooting Low-Fit or Focus / 105

   The Dishonest Shooter / 105

   The Honest Shooter / 105

   Right Handed/Right Master Eyed Shooter Shooting to the Right of a Point of Concentration—Gun Hand Too Small for the Grip on the Handgun / 106

   Right Handed Shooter Shooting to the Left or a Left Handed Shooter to the Right / 107

      Reason #2 for a Right Handed Person to Shoot to the Left of a Point of Concentration—Lack of Fit, Lack of Skill / 107

Strength / 108

   Strength on the Grip / 109

   Improperly Gripping the Handgun / 109

   Properly Gripping the Handgun / 109

Pulling the Revolver Trigger / 110

   Homework / 111

Pulling a Semi-Auto's Trigger—Double Action Only / 112

Concentration / 113

Arjuna the Archer / 114

   Another Story About Arjuna / 116

Testing Your Level of Concentration / 116

The Psychological Processes of Consistency / 117

Targets / 118

   The Paper Target / 118

   The Steel Target / 119

Fitting the Handgun to the Shooter / 123

   Programming the Fit / 123

Option 1 / 123
Reprogramming the Subconscious / 123
Option 2 / 124
Option 3 / 125
A Learning Experience / 127
Range Activity / 128
   The Pointing Position / 128
      A Modified Isosceles Arm Position / 129
      A Basic Body Position—Modified Isosceles Arm Position / 129
Taller Than Normal Shooter / 130
Beginning to Learn—Shooting the First Box of Ammunition / 130
150 Rounds of Fire Later—A New Member of the Club / 131
A Beginning Handgun Shooting Sequence / 132
Exercise to Sharpen the Eye of the Shooter / 133
Walk and Draw Sequences / 134
The Fighting Stance / 134
Learning to Shoot from Any Position the Body Could Be In At the Time Lethal Force is Necessary / 135
Multiple Targets / 138
   Shooting on the Move / 138
   Speed of Fire / 138
Pursuit and Shoot Sequences / 139
   An Awesome Feat / 140
Accuracy in Point-Shooting / 140
Tightest .45 Caliber Group / 142
Effective Distances in Point-Shooting / 149

Shooting at Night / 150
Potential Nighttime Accuracy / 151
A Nighttime Sequence / 154
Mindset / 154
Shooters Games / 155
   Snakes / 155
   Ants / 156
The Instructors Memories / 157
Border Patrol Memories / 161
Eagle Pass Drug Seizures 2000 / 163
Maurice Dixon and Warren O'Neal Incident / 164
   Azrack-Newton Abduction-BPA Murders / 167
   Alan W. Gordon Shooting Incident / 169
   East Desert Shoot-Out / 172
   Jewel Valley Shootout / 177
   Bob Gilbert Shooting / 180
   Gordon Schneider Incident / 181
   Loma Linda Ranch Episode / 183
   A Tale of the Tiger / 186
   Shooting Incident Vega Verde Area / 192
The Life of a U.S. Border Patrol Agent / 194
   Day-to-Day Operations / 194
   A Drug Bust in Action / 198
"Hole-In-One Club" Membership / 201
Hole-In-One Members / 202

## Foreword

My law enforcement career has spanned eighteen years, first as a police officer in Texas and now as a U.S. Border Patrol Agent. I entered on duty with U.S. Border Patrol (USBP) in San Diego, California. After serving five years in California I transferred back to Texas where, for the past nine years, I have had the privilege of being a certified firearms instructor for the USBP. I have also had the privilege of instructing firearms training at the USBP Academy at Charleston, South Carolina.

My first introduction to point-shooting techniques was at the Del Rio Police Departments gun range in Texas many years ago where one of the department's instructors touched on it briefly. So briefly, in fact, that I never really gave it much thought until years later. My perspective on point-shooting at the time was somewhat likened to that of the use of smoke and mirrors in a carnival show, or the shooting in an old western B-movie. I didn't really understand its full potential, nor did I believe one could really master it.

After entering on duty with the U.S. Border Patrol, I attended the academy at the Federal Law Enforcement Training Center (FLETC), Glynco, Georgia. The training I received there is still the most grueling, intense and most rewarding I have ever received in my life. The firearms instructors at FLETC who instructed my session were all expert shots. I also had the privilege to receive instruction from the late John Jacobs. Mr. Jacobs knew how to drive a point home to his students and at the same time he knew how to keep the class interesting. I have always said that if I could be half the instructor John Jacobs was, I would be a great instructor.

At FLETC, I was taught the importance of sight alignment and trigger control. I still remember the firearms instructors walking up and down behind the firing line yelling over and over, "Front sight, front sight . . . stay on your front sight only! Your target should be blurry!" Well, it worked. My shooting skills did improve. However, if I am to be honest, I must admit that in the back of my mind lay a bit of doubt. I always wondered were I ever face-to-face with a deadly force encounter, would I actually take the time to locate my front sight? I suspected that my answer would be a resounding, "NO, I WOULD NOT!" More than likely I would be fixated on my adversary and would have no clue as to where my front sight was.

I hoped that the simple repetitiveness of all those shooting sessions over numerous qualifications and training drills would automatically force a return to the correct shooting stance, sight-alignment and grip without any conscious effort of my own. I believed that trigger control alone would be the only thing I might still have control over. For several years I hoped that this would be enough. I convinced myself that all those hours on the firing line had to give me an edge over most adversaries. Well, that is in part true, but it is not necessarily enough.

One thing that I have learned during the years I've been teaching is that a law enforcement officer has to find a way to overcome any doubts he may have about his effectiveness with a firearm. There cannot be anything in the back of an officer's mind causing interference or distraction when that officer's life is imminently on the line. The officer has to have a high degree of confidence on his side. In the gambling profession this is called a "winning attitude"; almost arrogant, if you will. Early on in my law enforcement career, when I was a recruit at the police academy, I remember being told that if I was ever being attacked by an assailant, I had to become the aggressor in order to survive. I later found this to be true when I became a beat cop. The mere fear of getting injured or killed made me become the aggressor. I found that "winning attitude" that helped me in overpowering many of my assailants, even those who were twice as big as I.

Since a law enforcement officer willingly gambles with his life on a daily basis, he should have that same confidence and "winning attitude" in a gunfight. The will to survive and to overpower one's adversaries in a life or death struggle must be ever present in the officer's mind. There cannot be any room for any kind of doubt. An officer must have the confidence of his training, skill and dedication on his side . . . always.

I know that at times it seems that this is easier to say than to accomplish. For this reason, when we conduct firearms training at the Del Rio Sector range, we are constantly emphasizing to our students how important it is for them to train as close to reality as possible. In fact, we demand it.

In 1996, I had the good fortune of meeting Jim Gregg. I attended one of his courses emphasizing point-shooting skills with various firearms, marking the beginning of my experimentation and research of this technique. As it turned out, I was partly correct when I used to hope that my shooting posture and sight alignment would return to the same position as when I was sighting the weapon. They actually do, to some degree. However, I came to discover that if one maintained proper trigger control and remembered what Mr. Gregg referred to as one's "fit", one could draw and shoot on target each and every time.

After attending the course, I started experimenting with different point-shooting postures. I wanted to know if I could physically teach myself to find my "fit" in different positions. These positions ranged from shooting from hip-level positions to shooting from prone positions. They varied from two handed shooting to one handed; from a moving, standing-upright position to a stationary, crouching position. I also attempted point-shooting drills as I moved backward away from a target, simulating suppressive fire during a tactical retreat. All of these positions incorporated point-shooting techniques without the use of the pistol sights. I figured if I could teach myself these techniques, I could teach others. Well, I was very pleased with my results.

I finally put together a couple of courses for our Border Patrol Agents. I began to learn more about the technique simply by teaching it to others. The first course I put together encompassed six pistol magazines and seventy-two rounds of ammunition for each student. In any given class, I had groups of students who had attended Mr. Gregg's course along with new agents who had never even heard of Jim Gregg.

Those who had previously attended one of Jim Gregg's courses appreciated the opportunity to try the technique again. I discovered that many of them had, unfortunately, stopped practicing the technique. Since they had not utilized the training in some time, their confidence levels in point-shooting had declined. Surprisingly enough, though, their skills with the technique had not. They simply needed one of us to again "point" them (if you'll excuse the pun) in the right direction. They, too, seemed to be surprised that they could still fire their pistols accurately without using the pistol sights. To reiterate, the only thing I needed to do was to reinforce their confidence in the technique again.

For the students who had never taken any of Jim Gregg's courses, the technique was invaluable. A number of students appeared to be a bit skeptical when I first explained what we were going to do and what was expected of them. Their reaction reminded me of how skeptical I had been years earlier. A good number of them, however, seemed relieved when I explained to them that they would actually be fixated on their target as they shot and not on their pistol's front sight. Apparently, a lot of them had the same doubts that I used to have about staying on the front sight if engaged in an actual gunfight.

At the end of the training, even those agents with poor shooting skills seemed to be walking on clouds. Their confidence levels were so high that their faces were beaming. I got them to realize that by being so focused, there was little possibility of their missing since all their attention was drawn to the exact spot each time they acquired their target. They remembered their own appropriate "fit" and went back to the exact same position each time. They learned to trust that as long as they had good trigger control, their "fit" would not steer them wrong. They realized that their eye-hand coordination was a natural movement that they had been doing subconsciously all their lives.

I now regularly teach a point-shooting class based on Jim Gregg's techniques. My basic course of fire begins with 24 rounds fired from two magazines from a distance of about 10 yards. Both magazines are fired slowly in four to six shot groups, depending on how quickly the shooter grasps the concept of trigger control and correct "fit". With minor adjustments made by me, the shooter eventually finds his physical "fit" and accurately hits his target. When this occurs, my job is then to make the shooter freeze and have him remember how every part of his body feels in relation to his entire posture. I ask the shooter to note and remember how his wrists feel in relation to his forearms; how his forearms feel in relation to his shoulders; how his shoulders feel in relation to his waist, and so on. I ask the shooter to burn all this information to memory and to duplicate it again on his next draw. Hence, his "fit" is discovered and committed to memory.

With the next two magazines, also with 24 rounds from 10 yards away, I incorporate what I call the 1-2-3 Drills. A shooter will draw and fire one round at a target and then reholster. He will then draw again and fire two rounds and reholster; then, three rounds and reholster; then go back to one round and so on. The purpose of the drill is to eliminate what I call *"inevitable cheating"* with the first round. You see, what I have discovered is than when a shooter is first learning his "fit", he often fails to acquire it on the first shot. He'll draw and fire, realize that he is off somewhat to the left or right and makes the appropriate adjustments. Every subsequent shot thereafter hits its mark. That's what I call inevitable cheating. The shooter is actually cheating himself on the first shot. In an actual gun fight, that first shot may be the difference between winning or loosing the confrontation. Therefore, I decided that it is imperative that the student knows his "fit" just as well on the first shot as he does on all subsequent shots. The 1-2-3 Drills help in getting this point across.

The final part of my basic course deals with a moving posture, or moving "fit". I toss small, empty, plastic cartridge boxes on the shooting berm and have the students practice their point-shooting skills on these much smaller targets. I like to use bright red ones because they seem to catch the shooter's eye so much easier. However, that's just a personal choice. Green plastic soda bottles work well, too. The shooter's objective is to hit his target using his point-shooting skills. Once he does, the small box or bottle almost always flies into the air about four feet. The shooter must move his "fit" as a whole unit, keep his concentration on his moving target, and fire at it again as it lands on the berm. The target will again fly into the air and the shooter has to hit it as many times in a row as possible. The record thus far with my students has been six consecutive hits before missing. That agent took that green bottle from one end of the berm to the other, point-shooting all the way. Six times in a row he shot at that bottle and six times in a row it flew into the air before he missed. He was deservedly pleased with himself and his confidence in his shooting skills was extremely high that day. As his instructor, it was my turn to beam. I also incorporate multiple targets on the berm and instruct the shooters to fire at different targets in one draw.

Another objective for the shooter during this drill, is to observe how far off his mark he is when he does, in fact, miss. Usually, the misses are no farther than one or two inches from the intended target. Obviously, it is best to do this on a shooting berm composed of earth and soil so that the misses are easier to see. Once a shooter sees that he is hitting an object as

*Art Barrera (Right Front) Senior Patrol Agent and Lead Firearms Instructor, U.S.Border Patrol, Del Rio, Texas*

small as a cartridge box or a soda bottle from a distance of about 10 yards, or that he is missing it by only a couple of inches, his confidence levels reach a height that he has probably never enjoyed before. Have enough ammunition on hand after the seventy-two round drill is over because the shooters will want to do more shooting!

In my opinion, point-shooting techniques have proven to be viable tools that provide our officers an edge over adversaries they may encounter in the field. They are life-saving techniques that can be used in emergency situations, in confined spaces, in close quarter combat, and with the benefit of not having to assume the "perfect" firing stance that is used during so many qualifications in most training environments. Del Rio Sector's Chief Patrol Agent, Paul M. Berg, has said on many occasions that he supports any and all types of training and tools that will help save the lives of our agents who become involved in deadly force encounters. Point-shooting training techniques remain at the top of that list.

—Art Barrera, Senior U.S. Border Patrol Agent
Lead Firearms Instructor, Del Rio, Texas
Hole in One Club Member, January 3, 1997

# The Gregg Method of Fire Control

## A TRAINING MANUAL ON POINT SHOOTING

## SHOTGUNS

End of a perfect day—Jim Gregg and Billy Fay, 1972

## Early Experiences with Firearms

For the past 60-plus years I have had a forever love for guns and shooting. I'm not sure when my interest in shooting began. I think it was when I was 9 years old and looked into the window of the Lewis County Hardware Store and saw a side-by-side Daisy BB gun on display; it looked like a real double-barreled shotgun. The price tag read $5.00. That was a whole lot of money in those days. I was so interested in the BB gun, that each day after that first look I rode my bicycle two miles to town just to see it again. One day after watching me look through the window almost on a daily basis, the manager came out and asked me if I'd like to come in and see the gun. I couldn't wait and when he gave it to me it became one of my life's greatest experiences. I finally gave it back, but each day thereafter, I continued to ride the two miles to town just to look at it. On the twenty-fourth day of December, 1936 it was wrapped and under the Christmas tree.

I really enjoyed going to visit my Uncle Johnny's on Sundays and shooting the BB gun. Uncle Johnny had a farm in the country. There always seemed to be a skunk under the old farm house as the inside always smelled like one. I really liked to shoot the BB gun and did so, until a couple of years later, it didn't work any more. About that time I became interested in Uncle Johnny's .22 caliber rifle. Ammunition for the .22 caliber cost more than BBs; .22 shorts were 18 cents for a box of fifty and .22 long rifle cartridges were 22 cents a box. Money was tight during the Depression but I found that collecting empty beer bottles and selling them provided the money to buy ammunition for the twice-a-month trip with my dad to my Uncle Johnny's.

Shooting the BB gun and the .22 caliber rifle accurately was a natural process of seeing my target, not being in a hurry, bringing the stock to the face, setting the sights to where I wanted the shot to go and pulling the trigger smoothly. If I did it right, I normally hit my target. If I didn't do it right, I generally missed and I didn't like to miss. I received a lot of enjoyment from being able to hit what I wanted to hit and along the way maybe learning something about shooting straight.

When I was 14 years old I got my first shotgun. It was a 12 gauge, Montgomery Ward Western Field. It was a pump gun and I liked it. With repetitions I learned to pump it smoothly for a needed second shot at a mallard rising out of Dillenbaugh Creek. One thing I always did subconsciously was to have my eye on the target and put the shot where I expected the target to be. At the time I didn't think much about a right or wrong way to shoot a shotgun; I just shot it and generally I got what I shot at if it was in range. That's the way I shot a shotgun; I didn't have to think about it. I guess it was just a natural function.

I continued to shoot the Western Field shotgun for about 2 years, but one day I broke the slide rod that connects the forearm to the bolt. I had it fixed and continued to shoot it but it wasn't long before the slide rod tip broke again. I had it fixed for the last time and then traded it, and more money, for a Model 12 Winchester. I took the new shotgun home and put it together. When I brought it to my face, however, my eye was not looking down the barrel the way I looked down the barrel of the Western Field. Not giving this relationship a whole lot of thought, I decided to take my new Winchester hunting. The first pheasant that got up I shot at and missed. Sometime later, a second pheasant got up and flew straight away; I shot again and missed again. I went home and thought about the difference between looking down the barrel of the new Model 12 compared to looking down the barrel of my first shotgun and decided to make a change in the stock of the Model 12.

I got on my bicycle and went to town to buy a wood rasp and sand paper. Back home again, I'm sure I closed my eyes as I made the first pass on the comb of the shotgun where I sat my face when wearing my hunting coat. I continued to carefully cut and sand down the comb until I could see down the barrel just the way I looked down the barrel of the Western Field with my hunting coat on.

The next day after school my borrowed hunting dog and I walked down the street we lived on until we arrived at one of my favorite hunting spots. I had not been hunting long until the first pheasant got up, I shot and it crumbled to the ground and the springer spaniel retrieved it. I stowed it in my hunting coat and we went on hunting. Just before quitting time the dog started working a bird and very soon another rooster got up, I shot and it, too, crumbled and fell to the ground. My faithful companion retrieved it and I had a pair of pheasants and a shotgun I could hunt with knowing that it would shoot where I pointed it. A gun fits if it shoots where you are looking. Since being that 16-year-old duck and pheasant hunter, I've had thousands of shots at game birds and have found that if I get a little excited and take the excitement into that period of time I'm pulling the trigger, I normally shoot in the area of the target. Paying attention to business and having total concentration and focus on the target is my biggest challenge in shooting straight with a weapon that shoots where I point it.

In 1958, at the age of 31, my seasonal shooting changed when I got an invitation to shoot trap and skeet at the Boeing Gun Club. I had heard of these clay target games but never gave it much thought as facilities in the Pacific Northwest were few and far between. The invitation was extended by a friend who also worked for the Boeing Company. The next Saturday we met and went out to the gun club. My friend liked to shoot skeet, so I signed up for a round. My friend explained the game of skeet to me and we began to shoot. When we finished I ended up breaking twenty-three out of twenty-five targets and I really had a lot of fun. My friend told me that I should think about shooting in the club championship the following weekend. I told him I'd like to and showed up the following Saturday and signed up to shoot.

In my squad was the preceding years' Club Champion. He had lots of patches on his vest, which told me he was a very good shot. There are five shooters in a squad and the champ was the number one shooter, I was the number two shooter, etc. The champ and each member of the squad began shooting at Post number one, (High House). The champ and I were both straight until we arrived at Post number five. The champ walked up to the post, reached into his pocket for two shells, but when he went to load his over-and-under shotgun, he fumbled a shell and it dropped to the ground. He immediately bent over and picked up the dropped shell, loaded it and called for the High House target, and shot behind it. He then called for his optional shot, hit the target, and then called for the low house and hit it. We finished the very important round of skeet with Jim Gregg being the new 1958 Boeing Dog and Gun Club Skeet Shooting Champion with a twenty-five straight.

Lots of times I've thought about that first competitive shoot. By bending over to pick up that shell on Post number five, the champ's eyes would not focus clearly until his head cleared. He simply shot when he was not mentally ready to shoot. The mind controls the eyes, the eyes control the hand, the hand controls the gun, and the gun controls the bullets so, aren't we really controlling the bullets with the mind?

# Developing the Gregg Method of Fire Control

## Seattle Gun Club

In May 1963 I hired on as the manager of the Seattle Gun Club in Redmond, Washington. The club facilities were run down; everything had to be fixed and painted. Traps had to be cleaned, weeds mowed, and, eventually, we had a first-class gun club. I loved the work, the pay was poor, but the environment was great and I could shoot anytime. I became a proficient skeet shot, Class AA in 12 and 20 gauge and Class A in 28 and 410 gauge. Trap shooting was my favorite, and I liked to compete. I shot Class AA in 16 yard trap and I shot at the 24 yard line at handicap yardage.

From May 1963 until the fall of 1969 life was routine, but one day in September 1969 the phone rang and Howard S. Wright, the builder of the Space Needle in Seattle, was on the other end of the line. He asked me if it would be possible to bring a fellow to the gun club to hold a shooting school. At that time, I didn't give any lessons in shooting. For the past three years, Holland and Holland shooting schools, from England, would send an instructor to the Seattle Gun Club to hold lessons in shotgun shooting, but no one gave lessons in the Fall of the year just before hunting season, so I told Mr. Wright it would be okay to hold a shooting school.

The scheduled first day of the shooting school arrived and so did the instructor. He was a short man from Columbus, Georgia, and his name was Lucky McDaniel. Lucky was a very likeable fellow who talked all the time and my first impression of him was very good. When it came time to work with the first student of the day, Lucky left the clubhouse with his son Butch, the student, and a Daisy Model 96 air rifle with the sights on the front and the back of the barrel removed. I thought, "What is going on here?" From a distance I watched Lucky explain to the student how to bring the stock of the BB gun to his face, and set the lips the same height as the comb on the stock, which would put his the line of sight about 1½ inches above the plane of the barrel. With this simple introduction to shooting, the student seemed to be ready for the first target. Butch then held up an aluminum washer, 3/16 inches thick and 3½ inches in diameter with a ¼-inch hole in the center. Lucky told the shooter not to just look at the thrown washer, but to focus the top of the washer when ready to shoot. Lucky's son Butch then threw the target into the air, flat side facing the student. The student did what he was told to do and he hit the washer with a BB. The sequence was repeated and the student hit the washer again and again, and it quickly became repetitious in that, if he did what Lucky initially told him to do, then he always hit the target. The washer was soon changed to a smaller washer 2½ inches in diameter with a ¼-inch hole in the center, and, if by chance, the shooter did miss the target, Lucky said "You shot right through the hole in the target."

Lucky's student continued with the shooting lesson by first bringing the butt of the stock to the shoulder pocket, stock to the face, and focusing out to where he expected the target to be. Butch would throw the aluminum target into the air, about five feet away facing the shooter. The shooter saw the target, focused the top of the target, and pulled the trigger and the washer would ring with another hit. This shooting sequence was repeated again and again and it became simple to hit a smaller target thrown into the air with an air rifle without sights. How the shooter saw the target was always the same: anything in the air, focus the top leading edge and fire!

After this initial introduction to *instinctive shooting**, Lucky sometimes asked the student for a quarter, then he threw it into the air and, with the student's point of concentration at the top of the quarter, the student normally hit it. Many times Lucky spun a dime into the air and the student hit it. As an observer, I was impressed with this very unusual introduction to shotgun shooting.

At this point in the shooting lesson, Lucky generally took a coffee break and then got back to the skeet field with a 12 gauge Remington, Model 1100 skeet gun without a bead on the end of the barrel. Lucky would then

---

*Instinctive shooting is what Lucky McDaniel called a method of training people to shoot a shotgun.

have the student bring the shotgun to the face, then look out to see where the first target would be thrown and when it is thrown, focus the top leading edge of the clay target and pull the trigger. Butch then threw one 10 to 15 yards in front of the shooter; the barrel moved to the target, the shot fired and the target was powdered. The next target was thrown, the sequence was repeated, and the results were the same. At this point students found that by doing certain things, they always hit the target. By deviating from a standard, they most likely missed their target, and each shooter always knew before the shot was fired that the shot would be a miss. The feedback is subconscious and is based on a relationship between the focal point of the eye relative to the point of impact at the time the subconscious mind pulls the trigger.

Lucky McDaniel didn't have any "Try Gun." He did no measuring of the stock to speak of. Every now and then he looked around on the ground for a pull-tab off a pop can so he could check the position of the shooter's controlling line of sight. The one-hour lesson for $35 with a coffee break was the best lesson in shooting a shotgun the students ever had. The average shooter easily broke twenty-three out of twenty-five targets, and there were times a student broke 100 straight on hand-thrown targets.

One of the best examples of learning came in October 1969 when Chuck Dryke took a lesson in shooting from Lucky McDaniel. After the lesson Chuck went back to his Sunnydale Shooting Club and began to teach his 8-year-old son Matt how to shoot a washer out of the air with a BB gun. Matt took to this activity like a duck takes to water and by the time he was 9 years old he was shooting twenty-five targets straight with a 12 gauge Winchester semi-automatic that was too heavy for him. He would call for a target, lift the gun with the strength of a nine-year-old, break the target and drop the gun to a resting position. By the time Matt Dryke reached 14 years of age, he could break a twenty-five straight while riding a unicycle around the skeet field. The U.S. Army signed him up after high school, and he became a member of the Marksmanship Team at Fort Benning, Georgia. When he was 21 years old, Matt Dryke won a gold medal at the Olympics in International Skeet.

# Teaching Point-Shooting the Shotgun

In October 1969, I began to teach what was then referred to as Instinctive Shooting. At first I ran into problems in teaching some people how to shoot a washer out of the air with the BB gun. It was not a difficult feat, but some people had an awful time learning how to do it. Through trial and error, I found that in almost all cases their inability to shoot straight was related to at least one of four things: their eye system; the fit of the gun; the psychological processes of consistency; or, the habit of looking at the bead on the shotgun instead of the target.

Late in October 1969 I got a call from a fellow who wanted a shooting lesson. I gave him a time and date and a few days later he showed up for the lesson. I went through my normal routine of introducing him to the BB gun, told him how I wanted him to see the 3½ inch aluminum washer, the washer was thrown and he missed. I cocked the gun, gave it to him, the washer was thrown and he missed. I repeated the sequence again and again, but the man just couldn't hit the washer. As a novice instructor in Instinctive Shooting, I really didn't know much about what I was doing, but the lessons I had given previously did follow a pattern. I thought I knew a little about what I was doing but this student presented a problem. My student finally said, after so many missed targets, "What am I doing wrong?" and I said "I really don't see why you are missing the target, but let's go have a cup of coffee!" On the way to the clubhouse, I began to think about something Lucky did every now and then and that was to stop and look around on the ground for a pull-tab off a pop can. When he found one he gave it to the shooter, and told him to hold it out at arm's length and line it up with Lucky's right eye. Lucky then looked back through the pull-tab and saw something—I didn't know what. Then he most generally moved the shooter's head to the right or, in many cases, suggested that the gun be operated from the opposite shoulder. After a change to the opposite shoulder, and a few practice repetitions of bringing the gun to the face, the 3½–inch washer was thrown and, glory be, the shooter hit the target most of the time.

Knowing nothing about what Lucky was seeing when he gave the pull-tab to his student, I wondered if perhaps my problem was connected in some way to my new student not being able to hit his target. I looked around on the ground, found a pull-tab, gave it to my student, and had him line it up with my right eye with both of his eyes open. He did as I asked and the pull-tab lined up to his left eye. I thought for a minute and the answer came, he had to be crossfiring! *A gun fits if it shoots where your looking; a gun fits it it shoots where you point it and it fits if it supports the controlling line of sight that's looking at where you want the shot to go.* I quickly saw that the plane of the barrel did not support the left eye's controlling line of sight, so I had my student switch the gun to the left side, his weak side. This is a most difficult change to make and the older you get the harder it is! After moving the air rifle to the left side and having the shooter move the gun up to his cheek and down several times, I thought we were ready to shoot. The 3½-inch washer was thrown and he hit it. Again the target was thrown and he hit it. We continued until my shooter's mind was totally off having to shoot from his weak side. I changed the size of the washer to 2½ inches and it made no difference in his skill as long as he continued to see his target the same as he did a larger target. My student then went from shooting washers out of the air with the air rifle to the 12 gauge Model 1100 shotgun and he broke more targets than he ever did in his life. It ended up just great because I had $35 for the lesson, my student was overjoyed. Plus I learned that there is a lot more to teaching shotgun shooting than a target, a gun, and a shooter. From that day on I never had a student begin shooting unless I checked to see how the student would see a target with both eyes open.

## Eliminating the Air Rifle as a Step between the Shooter and the Target

After teaching point-shooting the shotgun with the use of a Daisy air rifle and various sized washer targets for two years, one day I found myself in a predicament. It was a Saturday morning at the gun club and in walked a man who wanted a shooting lesson. I told him that I couldn't give a lesson on a Saturday as that was a shooting day for the club. He explained that he just had to have a lesson as he was going hunting with several of his friends and didn't know a thing about shooting the shotgun. My wife said to me, "We aren't very busy with club activity, so why don't you take the fellow out and give him a lesson?" I explained that I needed her assistance in throwing the metal target to shoot at. She responded, "Why don't you take the fellow out and do the best you can without the use of the air rifle?" The fellow standing there said the same thing. So I said "Okay. Let's go." I gathered the Remington Model 1100 12 gauge shotgun, 100 rounds of target loads and, as I walked out to a skeet field, I wondered what I was going to say to the fellow about shooting the shotgun. and the answer came. I'll tell him the truth.

When we reached the skeet field, I talked about how to handle the shotgun. I then held up a clay target and told him how I wanted him to see a target (the top leading edge). I told him what I was going to do, and what I wanted him to do. After a short introduction to each of these very important steps in shooting, I again showed him how to make the gun ready and then how to bring the shotgun to the final position in gun handling. I again told him what I was going to do, and what I wanted him to do and after that, I told him I didn't want him to do any thinking, as conscious thought dilates the eyes.

I had the shooter focus out beyond the weapon to where I would throw the first clay target and, when he looked ready, I threw the first target. He moved the barrel to it and, BANG, he hit it! I asked him to bring the shotgun back to ready, remount it to the face, and focus out to where I would throw the second target. I threw the target, he moved the shotgun to it, fired, and hit it right in the middle. I continued the same sequence until the first box of ammunition was empty and the fellow had shot at and broken twenty-five targets in a row.

After a short break I continued the same sequence of preparing the shooter to shoot but in throwing the second box of shells I gradually changed the direction I threw the targets away from the shooter. The shooter continued to hit each target and when he finished 100 rounds of fire he had missed only four. This was the first time that I ever gave a shooting lesson without using the air rifle as a step between the shooter and his target. I quickly knew the answer to eliminating the air rifle from my lessons, and that was to tell the truth about gun handling, vision, the psychological processes of consistency and point-shooting the shotgun.

As my student left for home I thought about all the lessons I had given using the air rifle as a media between the shooter and the target and laughed as I recalled an earlier experience that lead me to hold a shooting school at the Fresno, California Trap and Skeet Range. Before I left for Fresno, I knew I had to have some one who could throw the washers to shoot at with the BB-Gun.

I talked to a friend of mine named Bob "railroad" Reynolds who was an FBI agent in Seattle. He had a son that was out of high school and at the time, didn't have a job. I called Bob and asked if the boy would be interested in going with me to Fresno and helping me with the shooting lessons. Bob called back and said the boy would be delighted so I asked him to have the boy come out to the gun club and learn just how to throw the two metal washers.

A few days later we left for Fresno in my 1968 Ford truck for the two day drive to the gun club and we spent a week there holding a shooting school for one of the local sporting goods dealers. On the way home I thought about my profit and perhaps loss, having to pay for all the expenses: a nice motel, good food, gas etc. After arriving home, I figured it all out and the lad I took with me to throw the washers made more money than I did! It was then that I got to thinking about how great it would be to hold a shooting school without having to use the BB-Gun, I think this was the premier experience in teaching shotgun shooting and it all happened by just telling the truth.

## Learning to Point-Shoot the Shotgun

When I was a little fellow, my grandpa said that when I turned 14 years old (a good average age to begin shotgun shooting) he would teach me how to handle a shotgun. He died when I was 9. I never knew what he was getting at until I turned 30 years of age.

Any method of handling the shotgun is correct if the end result is excellent shooting. It's next to impossible to be a perfect shooter simply because we are human. When I first began to teach shotgun shooting to law enforcement, I taught gun handling the same way I taught it to people who wished to learn field shooting. I would show a shooter many ways to carry a shotgun safely, how to make it ready to shoot, how to bring it to the face to set the controlling eye in its proper relationship to the plane of the barrel, how to see a target and, last but not least, when to pull the trigger.

I would then check to see what kind of eye combination they had, and if they had any combination other than a master eye, I told them to close the opposite eye as the stock is brought to the face. I would then tell the shooter to bring the shotgun to the final shooting position, what I was going to do, and what I wanted them to do. After that, I'd tell them that I didn't want them to do any thinking! I emphasized that shooting must be done in three steps: First, we must see the target; second, we focus the top of the target; and, third, pull the trigger.

I would then throw the first target. The shooter would see it, bring the shotgun to it, focus the top of the target and fire the shot and the target would explode. I would then throw a second target, the shooter would repeat the sequence and the second target would explode, then slowly I would throw the third target, the fourth and the last target and the shooter generally would break all five. If, however, the shooter started thinking about how great they were doing, they will shoot under the next target thrown. "Conscious thought dilates the lines of sight and makes the hand and the barrel go down". Each time this happens the shooter will always know before the shot is fired that they are going to miss.

The next person who wished to shoot will go through the same initial steps in handling the shotgun. I'd re-check to make sure the shooter could shoot with both eyes open, I would show the shooter how to bring the gun to the ready position, how to bring it to the face, how to see down the barrel, then I'd throw the first target. The shooter would move the barrel to the target but not through the target, focus the top of the target and pull the trigger BLAM! The target is reduced to dust. I then would throw the second target BLAM, then slowly I would throw the third, the fourth and the last target and if the sequences were done without conscious thought on the part of the shooter, all targets would be broken. Learning is done by repetitions by telling yourself what you want to do, and then doing it. The number of repetitions required to learn anything depends on the complexity of what we wish to learn. It's a matter of teaching the subconscious what you want it to do and then letting it do it, then the act of shooting becomes subconscious and instinctive and that is the way it has to be before we know how to shoot or do anything else.

## Monkey See–Monkey Do!

In any class of shooters, directions to one shooter apply to all shooters. If I prepare the first shooter to shoot a thrown or a stationary clay target, I'm really programming all shooters in a class to do what the initial shooter is asked to do. If I prepare one shooter to shoot and the shooter hits all thrown targets, the next shooter will not want to deviate from what I've told the first shooter for fear of missing a target.

Years ago, I held a school for the S.W.A.T. team, Fort Worth, Texas, Police Department. In the shotgun portion of training, I set up the first shooter with proper steps in making the shotgun ready to shoot, mounting the shotgun to the final position in gun handling, and understanding the psychological processes of consistency, etc. We began the training by shooting hand-thrown clay targets. Very slowly I threw the first target, then the second, the third, fourth and fifth and all targets were normally broken. I then set up the next shooter with the same program and we began shooting and all targets were broken. The sequence of preparing each shooter to shoot, slowly talking each person into self- preparation to shoot and shooting with total concentration on the target resulted in a score of 248x250 broken targets. We all worked very hard to break as many targets as we broke and I was very happy.

We finished up the shotgun portion by running each shooter through the S.W.A.T. team obstacle course, which was spread out over a distance of well over 100 yards. The shooter ran with an empty shotgun, and on the return trip the empty shotgun was exchanged for one loaded with five rounds of target loads. The shooter maintained running speed to where I was standing, brought the shotgun to ready, then to the final shooting position as I threw the first of five targets into the air, one at a time, and when all ten shooters had finished, only one target was missed out of fifty shot at.

I said "You guys really did great. I'm really proud of you." The fellow that missed the one target stepped forward and said, "I missed the one target and I want to do it again." So we loaded up a shotgun. The shooter took off with the empty shotgun, ran the entire obstacle course the second time, came back to where I was standing and aggressively shot at and broke his five targets.

During the 23 years that I threw clay targets, each shooter in a class always had the final challenge of breaking "Five on a Covey Rise." Each shooter and I would go on a simulated quail hunt. Our standard shotgun was an 18-inch or 20-inch Remington 870 police shotgun with only a simple bead on the end of the barrel, which I called "The Pointer." Or, they could elect to shoot with my 20-inch barrel with no bead on it at all. As we walked into the "quail field" I would say "dog's working a bird." The shooter would bring the gun to ready, we'd walk in for the flush, set the feet and I would rapidly throw five targets into the air at various angles in front of the shooter. The shooter would mount the shotgun to the first target thrown, break it and then, without removing the gun from the face or shoulder, break the rest of the targets, one quickly after the other. Because the speed of fire is controlled by the speed of focus, shooting is done quite rapidly. All targets must be broken or we would repeat the sequence again. In the end everyone always broke their five targets winning a school hat as their reward.

## Your Eye System and How It Relates to Accurate Shotgun Shooting

I know of no statement that has done more damage to the potential of shotgun students than to say "If you're going to shoot a shotgun, you should do it with both eyes open. One eye open is aiming, two eyes open is pointing." Most everything we do, we do in response to what we see. The rest of what we do, we do in response to what we hear, taste, smell and feel, but the main sense is vision. Vision and the understanding of our vision and how we use it is the key to accurate shooting.

Several years ago I was holding a school for instructors at the Dallas Police Range. The evening of the second day we took a break for dinner and when we arrived back at the range, all the lights were on at the pistol range. I asked why they were burning so much electricity and the fellows told me that they were working to get a lady officer qualified. I asked why such a waste of energy to get one person to qualify with a shotgun, and they said she had tried several times without success. I decided to stick my nose into the instructors' business.

I walked over to where they were and politely said, "Hello, can I be of help?" The lady gave me a bad look, but the instructor was pleasant and said, "Sure, if you can help." I asked him if he had checked her eyes, and he said no. I picked up a small stick off the ground and gave it to her. I first asked her if she was shooting with both eyes open and she said yes, as that was what she was told to do. I explained how I wanted her to hold up the stick vertically and to line it up with my right eye. With both her eyes open, the stick came up. I noted that it was lined up with her nose. I had her bring the stick down and do the same thing again, and each time it lined up with her nose. This told me that she could see equally well with both eyes.

I explained how over 15 percent of people see as well with one eye as they do with the other, and, in those cases, the origin of their controlling line of sight lies halfway between the eyes. When these right handed people shoot a shotgun with both eyes open, the shot almost always goes to the left of the target. For this reason I asked her to close her left eye as she brought the stock of the gun to the face so that she could look straight down the barrel. I also told her that the shotgun was not designed with women in mind and the comb is normally too low for the average female shooter. I had her drop the stock on the face until she was looking straight down the barrel to where she wanted the shot to go. She immediately wanted to shoot. Without hesitation, she loaded four shells into the magazine, loaded the chamber, set her feet at a 45 degree angle to where she intended to shoot, closed her left eye as she mounted the shotgun to her cheek, and, when the smoke cleared, she had qualified beautifully with five perfect shots.

How accurately we catch a ball or hit a ball is controlled by how we see the ball. How accurately we shoot a handgun or shotgun is controlled by how we see our target and having a gun that shoots where we point it. To shoot a shotgun, see the target, bring the barrel up to support the controlling line of sight, set the pointer to where you want the shot/s to go, pull the trigger. All these steps become subconscious quickly because they are simple and, therefore, require few repetitions to make each step subconscious.

The speed of fire is controlled by the speed of focus. If shots are fired before we properly see the target, accuracy is lost. If we do not fire after we properly see our target, the conscious mind gets to thinking, the eyes dilate and accuracy is still lost.

*If your thinking about something I've said, you won't hear what I'm saying and you won't see me in focus. Conscious thought dilates vision and affects our ability to hear!*

## Physical or Psychological Errors

Errors in shotgun and handgun shooting are either physical or psychological. In learning to shoot any weapon, we must first address the physical part of shooting, then we can address the psychological processes of consistency or, more simply, the condition the conscious mind is in at the time shots are fired. The conscious mind should be empty during the period of time the weapon is firing. I have read that the average gunfight lasts 2½ to 3 seconds, the average number of shots fired are three. The final test of training will last about 3 seconds; this is the most critical period of time in an officer's life. What happens before the gunfight might well be excitement, fear and a million other things that can drastically affect the officer's ability to shoot straight. It is basic and advanced firearms training for the real thing that is so important in preparing the officer for duty.

# The Basics in Handling the Shotgun

Anytime we have a long gun in our possession, we'll have it in one of three positions:

the Carry Position;

the Ready Position;

and the Final Position.

# The Carry Position

Shotguns should be loaded in a hot standby condition—Four shells in the magazine, hammer down, safety off.

A Carry position is normally used to transport the long gun from point to point and should be used when the shooter is in Condition White, a relaxed condition we live in most of the time.

Fig. 2. The "Hands Free Sling" Carry.

Fig. 1. Shoulder Sling Carry.

The "Hands Free Sling"* provides a long gun carry position leaving both hands free to work suspects, ride an ATV, motorcycle or horse. The sling is adjustable to any size person whether shooting from a sitting, kneeling or prone position.

*The "Hands Free Sling" can be purchased from the: **River Bend Trading Co. P.O. Box 4076, Gleed Station, Yakima, WA 98904**

The **Hip Carry** is just another way to safely carry a long gun.

*Fig. 3. The Hip Carry Position.*

The **Port Arms Position** can be a resting position or an excellent position for moving quickly from one point to another. If the shooter should happen to fall while running, the weapon is protected from accidental discharge.

*Fig. 4. Port Arms Carry.*

In using the two carry positions shown in *Fig. 5* and *Fig. 6*, it is quick to move the shotgun from the carry to the ready position by lifting the support arm and moving that hand to the forearm, strong hand to the grip.

*Fig. 5. Single-Hand Arm Cradle Carry.*

*Fig. 6. Two-Handed Arm-Cradle Carry.*

The **Suitcase Carry**—Probably used more than any other carry if no one is directly in front of the person carrying the shotgun.

*Fig. 7. The Suitcase Carry.*

Just another way to get the shotgun from point A to point B.

*Fig. 8. Shoulder Carry Position.*

POINT-SHOOTING SHOTGUNS + 43

Fig. 9. Backwards Carry—Used in walking behind another person

In conclusion, carry your long gun any way you wish, but carry it safely first, comfortably second and

*NEVER POINT YOUR GUN AT ANOTHER PERSON UNLESS YOU MAY HAVE TO SHOOT HIM!*

## The Ready Position

The ready position is used in *Condition Orange*.* In long gun handling the ready position is almost as important as the final position that you will be in when shots are fired. A proper ready will determine how the long gun will rise to the face to support the line of sight that is looking at where you want the shots to go. If you think you may need the shotgun, then bring it to the ready and leave it at the ready until its use is no longer expected.

When at the proper ready, the shooter has three points of communication between the shotgun and the body. These points are: the forearm, the grip, and the side of the body.

*Fig. 10. The Ready Position.*

---

*Condition Orange is a condition being into if use of a weapon is imminent. The shooter is very alert, shotgun is at the ready, shooter is looking for a possible target, and when it does appear, every motion of the shooter to shoot, should be subconscious.

## The Forearm

The shotgun's forearm lies in the palm of the opposite hand. Caution: If the back of the palm overlaps the rear of the forearm, there is a chance that in the pumping action the palm can be caught in the forepart of the receiver and it can pinch and break the skin. One bad experience will generally correct this problem.

Fig. 11. *The correct way to place the hand on the grip.*

Fig. 12. *The incorrect way to place the hand on the grip.*

### The Grip

It is especially important for the shooter to properly place the hand onto the grip of the shotgun *(Fig. 11)*. If all four fingers of the grip hand are placed behind the trigger guard *(see Fig. 12)* then, when the trigger finger is moved to the trigger, the space left by the movement of the trigger finger will likely place the hand too close to the nose. This can cause the back of the thumb to recoil into the nose when the shotgun is fired.

*Fig. 13. Keep the shotgun in this same ready position no matter where you are looking.*

## The Side of the Body

When holding the shotgun at the ready, the butt of the stock should be held slightly below armpit level with the butt resting against the body in front of the armpit. The intent is to set the butt in a position so that stock movement, when mounting the shotgun, is held to a minimum. The comb should move freely to the face avoiding a U-ee trajectory that the stock will make if the butt is further to the rear in the armpit.

When at the ready, hold the muzzle of the shotgun higher than the receiver of the shotgun because the eye is higher than the shoulder pocket. When mounting the gun, the motion should be such that neither the receiver nor the end of the barrel, move to support the controlling line of sight first. Both the receiver and the muzzle should move the same distance up to the line of sight, then, from the time you see the target until the time shots are fired, the intended point of impact will stay in focus. We want to end up with a figure-eight relationship between the line of sight to the target and the plane of the barrel supporting it.

Always bring the shotgun to the proper ready if you feel you may need to shoot. If you have the barrel of the shotgun pointing up into the air or if you have the end of the barrel pointing into the ground, you are not ready to make a skilled shot. In this case if you do hit anything, it will be more by accident rather than on purpose. Be ready and be a very good shot.

## The Final Position

The final shooting position is reserved for *Condition Red**. In this position the shooter will have four points of communication between the body and the shotgun: the two hands, the shoulder pocket, and the face. The shotgun is held perpendicular to the shoulder pocket to retain the butt of the stock during the recoil cycle.

*Fig. 14. Right master-eyed shooter shooting with both eyes open.*

---

*Condition Red—The target appears, the shotgun subconsciously moves from the ready to the final shooting position, focus the target, set the pointer to where you want the shot to go and FIRE!

## Mounting the Shotgun to the Face

Always bring the stock to the face; never bring the face to the stock. As the eyes stay on the target, bring the shotgun up to support the line of sight, as you set the butt of the stock into the shoulder pocket, set the pointer to where you want the shot to go, and fire!

*Fig. 15. Take the stock to the face; never take the face to the stock.*

As you bring the stock to the face, do it in such a way that the eyes' relationship to the plane of the barrel is the same each time. Bring the stock to the cheek and nestle it into the pocket under the cheekbone. This movement locks the shotgun into a position that assures the gun will shoot consistently where you point it. Multiple shots should stack the same point of impact if the line of sight stays on the initial point of concentration.

*Fig. 16. Taking the face to the stock.*

If you mount the shotgun to the shoulder first, then bring the cheek down to the stock, the amount of skin stacked onto the comb can vary. The more skin stacked onto the comb, the higher you raise the controlling eye; the higher the controlling eye, the more you increase the possibility of shooting high. Consistency in setting the stock to the face is obtained with practice.

## Chinning the Stock

If the shotgun has rifle sights and a standard stock, it will probably be necessary to modify the way the comb is presented to the face by chinning the comb. My navy commander used to say "Gregg, don't let a problem present itself." My feeling is that shotguns just weren't designed to have rifle sights; they were originally designed to point and kill game birds. Years ago some fellow got the idea to add sights to a shotgun and, in theory, "As long as all people sight all guns, then all guns would fit all people." To explain: If all people in the world had that perfect sight picture when they fired their gun, then wouldn't all bullets for all people go into the same hole? The answer is Yes, but, the average fellow is not a good shot with the shotgun.

To check to see if you may have a problem in point shooting a shotgun with rifle sights on it, mount the shotgun to the face, set the cheek to the comb, then take a look down the barrel at what you see. If you're looking just over both front and rear sights to where you want the shot to go, then the fit will be very close or right on. If you're looking into the back of the receiver or looking into the back of a rear sight and the plane of the barrel has totally disappeared, then a fired shot is apt to go somewhere in the general area of the target—not a good feeling. Chinning the shotgun stock is a way of solving the problem. Chinning the stock can raise the line of sight very close to where it should be and still give the face a firm contact with the shotgun. Of course, you won't know for sure until you fire the shotgun. This method of adjusting the shooter to the gun is the only method of point-shooting a standard stocked shotgun with open sights.

## Female Shooters

The average female has a much smaller face and body size than the average male. When a female cheeks a shotgun that was stocked for a male, the end of the barrel will normally dip below the line of sight looking at a target. Then, if the back of the receiver breaks the controlling line of sight, the subconscious likes to pull the trigger and the shot will go low.

My job has always been to teach people how to shoot, but I can't unless the gun fits. People in the Border Patrol or any other law enforcement agency must shoot the gun their agency tells them to shoot. We cannot change the gun to fit the shooter, so we have to change the shooter to fit the shotgun. In order to do this with females, I used to add a 3/16 inch pad to the comb. In this way when a smaller faced person cheeked the stock, hopefully, they would see down the barrel just like the average male the shotgun was designed for. For me it was a win-win situation.

One day, however, a female shooter said, "This is not the shotgun I'm going to have in the patrol car; the gun we carry doesn't have a pad on the stock." I thought a bit and said, "Yes, you're right, but let's make a deal. Let me teach you how to shoot, and then I'll teach you how to shoot the shotgun you're going to have in the patrol car."

After the lady finished the basics of shotgun shooting, she picked up a duty shotgun without a pad on the comb and adjusted the stock downward on her face until she had the same relationship she had with the pad on the comb. Her skill continued to improve and I was happy and she was happy with the result.

I've thought a lot about why males tend to miss a target high and why females tend to miss a target low. I've ended up believing that from the time a shooter sees the target until the time the trigger is pulled, the line of sight to the target must not be broken by any part of the shotgun. In the case of the male shooters who normally miss high, I solve the problem by having the shooter move the pointer just to the target, but not through the target. If a female shooter is missing low, then I solve the problem by having her chin the stock to set the controlling eye the proper distance above the sights and then fire the shot/s.

For women, shooting with a plain barreled shotgun *(Fig. 17)*. First, focus the target, set the controlling line of sight the same distance above the plane of the barrel, set the pointer (bead) to where you want the shot go and fire!

*Fig. 17. Shooter with a plain barrel shotgun.*

For women using a peep-sighted shotgun, focus the point of impact, set the controlling line of sight the same distance above the front and rear sights, and fire!

*Fig. 18. Shooter pointing a peep-sighted shotgun.*

## Taller Than Average Shooters

These people can have a hard time shooting a standard shotgun because the stock, or "the length of the pull,"* will normally be too short. Consequently, the thumb of the grip hand is likely touching the nose in the final shooting position and shots fired can drive the thumb into the nose.

*Fig. 19. The shooter's nose is too close to the thumb and he will feel it when the shotgun is fired. (My 19-year-old grandson—6-foot 3-inches tall.)*

The distance between the thumb and nose can be shortened by the way the shotgun is mounted to the shoulder. If a shooter pulls the shoulder rearward, typically seen in target shooting the rifle, it will shorten the distance between the side of the thumb and the nose.

---

*The length of the pull is the distance between the center of the trigger and the center of the butt of the stock.

Fig. 20. A tall shooter with right elbow pushed forward to increase the distance between the thumb and the nose.

If taller than average shooters push the elbow forward as they mount the shotgun, the space between the nose and the thumb increases (*Fig. 20*). As a general rule, adult shooters should have a minimum ½–inch of space between the nose and thumb at the time shots are fired. I have, however, seen tall shooters shoot with the thumb against the nose and, with their concentration on the target, feel no recoil against the nose.

## Fitting the Shooter to the Shotgun

It is impossible to stock a shotgun so it will fit all people simply because all people are not the same size. There are tall people, short people, people of all shapes and sizes. In the U.S. the shotgun manufacturer stocks a shotgun so it will fit more people than if the stock was made to any other dimension. A well-made standard stock is one that sets the average face in such a way that the controlling eye sees straight down the barrel to the target without obstructions.

Shotguns are built for male shooters simply because men are the ones who most generally buy shotguns. The Remington Model 870 Police plain-barreled shotgun is stocked to fit people 5 feet 9 inches tall who weigh between 175 to 190 pounds and have an average face size. If a shooter is smaller than 5 feet 9 inches, then the odds are strong that the stock will be too long and the comb too low. If the shooter is taller than 5 feet 9 inches, then the odds are strong that the stock is too short and the comb too high.

Because the point of the comb is higher than the heel of the comb we can, within certain limitations, fit the shotgun to a person who is shooting low. We do it my moving the face forward on the stock to raise the controlling eye relative to the plane of the barrel. By raising the eye, we raise the point of impact. Shooters who use this method of raising the point of impact will need a minimum of ½ inch between the thumb and the nose to allow space so that the thumb doesn't recoil into the nose. If a shooter is shooting too high, then move the face rearward on the stock and lower the point of impact.

## Fixing a Shotgun to Fit Perfectly

Several years ago I got to thinking about the shotgun that fits just perfectly. There's an old saying that you only get one in a lifetime that fits perfectly and when you find it, don't sell it for a nicer looking shotgun unless you know how to make the new shotgun fit. A weapon of any type has three values: a monetary value, an aesthetic value, and a working value. The working value of a handgun or shotgun is the most important of the three.

Years ago I bought a Browning 20-gauge shotgun from a fellow. I shot a few rounds of skeet with it, I was happy with how it shot, and I liked the gun. In September of that year chukar partridge season opened in the state of Oregon so my friend, Andy, and I decided to go.

We traveled most of the night to Huntington, Oregon. In Huntington we had a great breakfast and headed back into the hills to see if we could find chukar partridge. We bumped along a rough road in my 1955 Volkswagon van, and it wasn't long until we had chukar running across the road in front of us. We bailed out of the VW and went for our shotguns and shells. I got my dog Cora out and while we were just finishing getting ready, Andy said "Cora's on point." I looked and sure enough she was on point. So I loaded the Browning 20 gauge over and under, took a few steps in the dog's direction, and up came a chukar.

It flew right toward me and I thought, "I'm in heaven." I brought the shotgun up to my face, put it to where I wanted the shot to go, fired the first shot, and never ruffled a feather. I fired the second shot and the results were the same. I couldn't believe this was happening! Andy was now laughing. I was a little upset and just couldn't figure out how the greatest shot in the world could miss such an easy target. I then brought the shotgun to my face, set the cheek, and looked for the end of the barrel—it was gone. I again brought the gun to my face, set the cheek, looked for the end of the barrel, and it was gone—the comb was too low.

I wondered, "How in the world can I fix the height of the comb clear back here in the hills of Huntington, Oregon." I thought about the first aid kit in the VW, which had Band-Aids in it, so I had Andy hold the shotgun while I laid on the comb one Band-Aid next to the other until I had a single complete layer of Band-Aids. I then brought the stock to my face, I cheeked the comb, and I was looking straight down the barrel. I finished my first aid to the comb by adding strips of plastic electrical tape on top of the Band-Aids until I had a nice smooth surface on top of the stock.

Andy, Cora and I took off hunting for some more chukar and it wasn't but a few minutes until Cora went on point again. Andy and I walked in and the air exploded with chukar. I shot a nice double, Andy got a double, and we were in business. I had a great weekend of hunting that never would have happened if it hadn't been for the Band-Aids and the knowledge of how to make a shotgun shoot where I point it.

# Correcting the Most Common Shotgun Shooting Problems

## Peeking

Peeking is having the habit of raising the head and cheek off the stock before a shot is fired. If this happens, subsequent shots will go high in direct proportion to the height of the eye over the receiver of the shotgun. Peeking has the same effect as raising the comb of a stock or raising the rear sight of a rifle, it will make you shoot high, so keep your head on the stock until after the shot has been fired.

The recoiling shotgun can have the same affect as peeking. The initial shot can cause the cheek to raise off the stock and if a second shot is fired, it will go high. If the cheek is reset to the comb and kept there, the second and subsequent shots should be as accurate as the first.

## A Right-Handed Shooter Shooting to the Left with Both Eyes Open

If a right-handed shooter has a common error of shooting to the left, close the left eye if it's open. It is very common to try to shoot with both eyes open, and if you do not have a master eye on the same side as the master hand, then you have a probability of shooting to the left. The probability of cross-firing is in proportion to the position of the controlling line of sight. So that, if a right-handed shooter has a dominant right eye *(See page 93)*, then the probability is 25 percent. If the right-handed shooter has eyes that are balanced in vision power, that is one eye sees just as good as the other, then they have 50-50 vision. The controlling line of sight lies half way between the eyes and the probability of crossfiring is 50% with both eyes open. I always have these shooters close the opposite eye as the stock is brought to the face.

If the right-handed shooter has a dominant left eye, then he has a 75 percent chance of crossfiring to the left. If the shooter has a master left eye and tries to shoot with both eyes open, he has about a 100 percent chance of crossfiring with the shotgun. Most people have corrected a problem such as this by changing the shotgun to the left or weak side, long before they get into law enforcement firearms training.

## Left-Handed Shotgun Shooter Shooting to the Right with Both Eyes Open

If a left handed person has any eye combination other than having a master eye on the same side as the master hand, I would suggest closing the right eye to solve a cross firing problem.

## Right- or Left-Handed Shooters Shooting High on Straight-Away Targets

If these shooters move the shotgun to and through a straight-away target, the odds are very high that a shot will go high. It must be remembered that the conscious mind does not pull the trigger after you learn how to pull it, it's the subconscious mind that pulls the trigger. To prevent shooting high from happening, move the out of focus muzzle or pointer just to the target but not through the target and fire. Then, from the time you see the target until the time you shoot the target, the target will stay in perfect focus.

If at this point you're still shooting high, cheek the stock a little more, lower the controlling eye and lower the point of impact. Now you're learning how to hold the shotgun so it shoots where you are looking.

## Open Sighted Shotguns

If the police shotgun is properly sighted in to point of aim it should shoot where aimed. If the same gun shoots high for certain people, the odds are strong that the shooter is raising the controlling eye relative to the rear sight as they point the front sight or pointer to where they want the shot to go.

This open-sighted shotgun is one of the most difficult to point because when open sights were added to the barrel the manufacturer never raised the stock a proportionate amount to the height of the sights added to the barrel. It would have been a very good thing if shotguns were restocked at the time sights were installed, then, the average shooter could set their face to the stock, look over both front and rear sights, set the pointer (front sight) to where they want the shot to go, and fire! With the same shotgun, shooters could use the sights for long shots (shooting slugs) by cheeking the stock just a little more in order to align the sights to where they want a slug shot to go, and pull the trigger: a simple system of aiming. With both methods of shooting, the eyes would still be on the target and no part of the weapon would be in focus.

## Peep-Sighted Shotguns

In law enforcement, if you're already under fire, it's very difficult to use a peep-sighted shotgun properly, which can lead to a spray and pray situation. When quarterly qualification time comes, however, using either open sights or peep sights properly can lead to perfect scores for everyone given time to use the sights and enough light to see through them. Looking through the aperture of the peep sight automatically centers the eye to the back of the barrel so you only have to set the front sight to where you want the shot to go, and fire!

Problems lie in using peep sights at nighttime if you're already under fire. When you try to look through that little bitty hole, things can get mighty confusing. When training at night with buckshot, bring the shotgun to the ready, put your eyes on the target, set the tritium pointer to the belly, and fire. In training, if the shot is right where you wanted it to go, you're okay. If the shot goes high, cheek the stock a little more, lower the controlling eye, and fire another shot. Setting the pointer to the belly of the target is insurance against shooting high while pointing a shotgun that is simply not built to point. If you set the pointer to the belly and shoot a little high, you win. If the gun shoots right on the money, you still win. Do what ever you have to do to win!

# Range Activity (Two Day Shooting School)

EQUIPMENT NEEDED
*(Per Person Unless Otherwise Noted)*

- 50 Rounds 12 gauge Target Loads
- 50 Clay Targets
- 15 Rounds Buckshot
- Ear and Eye Protection for Daytime and Nighttime
- 6 Police Shotguns Needed for a Class of 10 Officers (only half the class shoots at a time)

*Fig. 21. Single clay target holder.*

## Target Holders

People inherently like to break things, so I have always given them clay targets to break. It makes us feel good and it's a whole lot more fun than shooting a piece of paper.

I set the targets into a holder made out of ¾-inch OD, ½-inch ID steel channel *(see Fig. 21)* The holders are set into the top of a pointed ½×½×60 steel stake driven into the ground with a fence post driver.

## Training with Clay Targets

In a training sequence, each officer has a set of four targets to shoot. How the officer breaks a target will determine the fit of the shotgun. The learning curve is very short as shooters quickly learn how to cheek or chin the shotgun so it will shoot where they point it.

*Fig. 22. Shooters on the line.*

### Step #1

Before shooting begins I move to each shooter and check the way the shotgun is held at the ready position and how the shooter will mount the shotgun. I make corrections, if needed, and move to the next shooter until I've checked them all *(Fig 22)*.

*Fig. 23. Gun Handling. There is nothing better than hands-on training!*

## Step #2

Load all shotguns in a *hot standby condition*. Border Patrol hot standby condition is:

- Chamber empty
- Hammer down
- Safety off
- Four shells in the magazine.

*Fig. 24. The shot went high!*

## Step #3

I move to the first shooter in the line and have the shooter move through the following sequence.

- Bring the gun to ready, load the chamber, mount the stock to the face, bring the barrel up to the target, but not through the target, and fire. BLAM! Chamber the second shot.
- Bring the shotgun back to ready, mount it up to the face, bring the barrel up to the target not through the target, focus the second target, and BLAM! Chamber the third shot.
- Bring the shotgun back to ready, mount it up to the face, focus the third target, and BLAM! Chamber the fourth shot.
- Bring the shotgun back to ready, mount it to the face, focus the fourth target and BLAM!

The slide should be left open, the shotgun is empty, and I move to the next shooter and repeat this same learning sequence until I've finished programming each shooter.

If a shooter shoots high and residue is left in the target holder, I ask the shooter to lower the point of impact. This is done on a rifle-sighted shotgun by raising the line of sight off the front sight, or, better yet, see the target the same distance just above the front and back sights, and fire the shot. When a clay target is shot properly, using target loads, it turns to black smoke if shooting from the 15-yard line.

Raising the line of sight off a ramp front sight in order to lower the point of impact is a little difficult. It feels strange to shooters but, after three or four shots and after hitting a clay target in the middle instead of shooting high, shooters begin to see less and less of the shotgun. Targets become more and more clear—clearer than they have ever been—and confidence soars.

After each shooter on the line shoots four targets, I repeat the learning process by having all shooters load four shells in the magazine, hot standby condition. I then return to one of the first shooters on the line and have them bring the shotgun to ready, load the chamber, mount the shotgun to the face, focus the target, and fire the shot. Each target is shot as a single target, then the next until all four shots are fired. This same sequence is repeated by each shooter on the line.

*Fig. 25. Four targets for two shooters in a multiple target sequence.*

At this point if I have a shooter who is shooting high, I might get a few rounds of fire and go through the process with that shooter of lowering the point of impact until the eye of the shooter is well off the front sight a proportionate amount to where the line of sight is above the rear open sight or peep sight.

All shooters load four rounds, hot standby condition, bring the shotgun to ready, load the chamber, mount the shotgun to the face, and break one, two, three and four targets. Each target is shot as a single, two singles is a double, three singles a triple, etc. All shooters are now shooting, and in about four or five seconds the range is quiet again. I look down the line of twenty target holders to see if I see any residue in the bottom of the target holders. If I do, then I tell those particular shooters to lower the point of impact. They always give me a funny look because they have forgotten how. I explain it all again and, once the target is hit in the middle, it all seems so easy!

## Point-Shooting the Shotgun after a Pursuit

For safety, pursuits are made with the shotgun in a Hot Standby Condition. The chamber is loaded at the completion of the pursuit when ready to fire. Being able to fire a shotgun accurately after a pursuit is a very valuable asset to the officer. Consequently, for as long as I can remember, I have always ended a shotgun training session in the following way.

First, a single officer runs to the 30-yard line and returns to shoot four or five clay targets. Second, two officers run a distance of 80 or so yards before setting the feet and shooting multiple targets. Third, half the class runs to the 50-yard line and returns to shoot four or more targets, and it is rare that any shooter will ever miss his targets. Sometimes a small amount of residue will be left in the target holder, but this is not a missed target.

I believe competition between shooters is good for everyone. It sharpens skills and teaches the officers what they have to do to shoot very well. Breath control is not mentioned as the human body instinctively stops breathing during the critical period of time the weapon is firing.

*Fig. 26. Another multiple target set up for three shooters. I generally have half the class shoot at a time. The other half learns by watching and listening.*

POINT-SHOOTING SHOTGUNS + 69

Fig. 27. Target on the left shot too high. Target on the right is shot a little high. Shooter should raise their controlling line of sight off the front pointer and lower the point of impact further until the target is hit in the middle.

## Learning to Lead a Target

The following is the learning sequence I use for teaching shooters how to lead a target.

- Load four rounds in the magazine, Hot Standby Condition.
- Starting on the right side of the targets, bring the shotgun to the ready, load the chamber, mount the shotgun to the face, focus the first target, move the shotgun away from the line of sight, and shoot the second target.
- Bring the shotgun back to ready. Mount the shotgun to the face, focus the third target, move the shotgun away from the line of sight, and shoot the fourth target.
- Bring the shotgun to ready, mount it to the face, focus the fifth target, move the shotgun away from the line of sight, and shoot the sixth target.
- Finish up by focusing the seventh target and shooting the eighth.

In learning to shoot a target moving from left to right, repeat the sequence. Starting from the left, bring the shotgun to the ready, load the chamber, move the shotgun away from the line of sight, and shoot the next target on the right etc.

The same sequence used in shooting a stationary target is used on a moving target. As long as the eyes stay on the target, then the speed of the target and the movement of the mounted shotgun become relative to each other. To shoot a moving target, bring the shotgun to ready, focus the target, mount the shotgun to the moving target, put the pointer where you expect the target to be, and pull the trigger. With repetitions, leading a target becomes subconscious and instinctive. You will reach a point in learning were you won't have to think about leading any more, your subconscious does it.

In shooting from a standing position to a moving target or in shooting from a moving position to a standing target or in shooting from a moving vehicle to a moving target, as long as the line of sight stays on the target, everything stays relative no matter the speed of either the shooter or the target.

*Fig. 28. Multiple target setup used to teach shooters how to lead a target to put the shot where they expect the target to be. Note: In shooting any size of shot pellets through a shotgun, the speed of the shot will be in excess of 1200 feet/sec. At this speed, I would focus the target and put the pointer just in front of the suspects nose and pull the trigger. The above targets are set to train duck hunters to shoot game birds at a distance of 25 to 40 yards. The amount we lead any target would depend on its speed, distance to the target and the angle it is flying at.*

# How Not To Lead a Target

The most incorrect way of shooting at a moving target is by sighting the shotgun ahead of a target, which puts the target out of focus at the time shots are fired. Many shooters begin shotgun shooting this way and, hopefully, they end up keeping their eye on the target and pointing the shotgun to where they expect the target to be. The habit of aiming the shotgun ahead of a target probably starts with learning to shoot with a BB gun or rifle. And, although, "*as long as all people sight all guns, all guns fit all people,*" I know of no good habits connected with sighting or aiming a rifle that apply to skillful shotgun shooting.

Several years ago I got a phone call from a fellow who wanted to learn to shoot a shotgun. He said his wife got tired of him sitting on the couch watching TV. When he arrived for the lesson, I talked about shotgun shooting, gun handling, how to see a target, whether he could shoot with two eyes open, etc., and soon it was time to break some targets.

The initial targets were straight away and they are easy to hit, and the fellow's confidence was just great after shooting the third box of shells. Then it was time to shoot slight angle crossing targets from right to left. I started with an incoming target and my student shot behind it. I threw another target and he shot the same distance behind it. I threw ten slight angle targets and he shot the same distance behind all the targets. The shooter was taking his eye off the target to look at the bead on the front of the barrel causing him to shoot behind the crossing targets. I asked him about his shooting experiences and he said he used to be on the U.S. Army Rifle Team, 30 years ago and hadn't done any shooting since. A good habit learned in one method of shooting does not necessarily carry over into another method of shooting. The solution in the above case is to get rid of the old habit, and that takes an awful lot of repetitions.

## Daytime Shooting-Single Targets with Buckshot

During the day, set your feet, bring the shotgun to ready, load the chamber, mount the stock to the face, set the pointer to where you want the shot to go, and fire!

*Fig. 29. A single steel target is used for all shotgun shooting with buckshot loads. Target is cleaned with a 4-inch paint roller after each shot.*

## Nighttime Shooting with a Plain-Barreled Shotgun with a Tritium Pointer (Bead)

This shotgun is easier to shoot and less complicated than any other shotgun/barrel combination. With the eyes on the target bring the shotgun to ready, mount the stock to the cheek, set the pointer to the belly, and fire! At night a Tritium pointer gives the shooter something to point and it builds immediate confidence.

## Nighttime shooting with sighted shotguns with a standard stock

Point these shotguns at night just like you would point them in the day time. With the eyes on the target, bring the sights up to support the line of sight, set the pointer (bead) to the belly of the target or where you want the shot to go and fire the shot. If the shot goes high, cheek the stock a little more and lower the point of impact until you learn how to hold the gun so it will shoot where you point it. Night shooting accurately is not difficult.

## Multiple Targets at Nighttime

When shooting at night, vision is lost after each shot fired. In shooting more than one target, the speed of fire is controlled by the time it takes to see each target to be shot. After firing the first shot, leave the stock to the cheek for any additional shots.

### Maintaining a Level of Proficiency by Visualization

Firing a weapon only substantiates a mental process. I believe that skill, once obtained, stays with us the rest of our lives. You can maintain a high level of proficiency by using visualization, which is what I've always done. If you are a police officer and know how to shoot then handling your duty shotgun or handgun, so they will shoot where you point them, will be subconscious. The only thing left to do in pointing the handgun or shotgun is the act of focusing where you want your shots to go and fire! You must win the fight before the gun leaves the holster, you must know what you have to do to win, and then you must do it without having to consciously think about it.

At this point it all boils down to whether or not you've been trained to shoot accurately in a situation that's most likely to occur within a distance of 15 feet. Visualizing this same situation, how you will react, how accurately you will point the gun against a fellow who probably never had a shooting lesson takes seconds of thought, before you go on duty.

Statistically, if a police officer gets into a shoot, the suspect normally shoots first. 95% of the time it will happen within 21 feet of the suspect. 70% of the time it will happen within 10 feet of the suspect, and most likely it will happen at night, train for this scenario.

Our level of concentration is that part of our shooting skill that has the highest probability of changing. Once this occurs, the dimension of the cone of fire will change. It all depends on your training and self maintenance of your training (visualization and a round of fire now and then, at the range). Not knowing what you have to do to shoot very well under combat conditions is the problem, so the more you know about close quarter point-shooting with the shotgun and handgun, the better off you will be.

## The Mind's Eye—The Eye of The Subconscious

Most people have never heard of the mind's eye or the eye of the subconscious. Those of us who drive a car can recall driving for miles along a road while thinking about so many things other than driving. When this happens, I think it's the eye of the subconscious that keeps us on the road while we daydream.

Years ago Senior Agent Mike Williams and I were headed for the El Paso Police Department. We drove through a poorly lit residential area. My friend suddenly looked 90 degrees to the left and said, "There're five wets under that street light." He made a sudden left turn, stopped, walked up to the group, talked a bit, brought them all back to our vehicle and loaded them into the back seat of the sedan. As we headed for the Border Patrol station to off load them for processing, I thought about what had happened. My friend and I were driving down a street, and he spots five aliens 90 degrees to his left side almost in the dark of night. How did he know they were illegal? I believe it was his mind's eye that saw them—the eye of the subconscious. Its field of view is 180 degrees.

The most astonishing experience I've had with the mind's eye happened in September 1969 when Lucky McDaniel came to hold shooting lessons at the Seattle Gun Club. One night several shooters and I were out behind the clubhouse along with Lucky talking about how to lead a bird. Lucky said, "You don't have to lead a bird." Fred Rahn said, "You do, too." Back and forth it went until Lucky changed the subject. A week later Fred Rahn came into the clubhouse anxious to tell Lucky that he had gone duck hunting after their initial conversation about leading a bird. Fred said that he shot two limits of mallards and didn't lead a bird; it was just amazing. Years later I thought about that leading-a-bird conversation and decided that they were both right, and they were both wrong. Lucky was right in that we do not consciously lead a target. Lucky was wrong in that you have to put the shot where you expect the target to be otherwise you'll shoot behind it. Fred was right in that you have to lead a bird to put the shot where you expect the target to be. Fred was wrong in that it is a subconscious lead that we learn by consciously leading targets at various angles, speeds and distances until you get a "feel" for leading and then it becomes subconscious. All "feel" feedbacks are subconscious.

During that argument behind the clubhouse, Lucky got off the subject by asking me to get the Daisy BB gun, a black marking pen, and a twenty-five-cent piece. Shortly, I returned and gave Lucky the quarter and the marking pen. He took the marker pen, started in the center of the quarter, and drew a line to the edge. He then held up the quarter and asked me to hit the line on the quarter with a BB. I looked at him and said, "You want me to hit the line on the quarter with a BB." He said, "Yes." I thought he was crazy, but I made the gun ready. He threw the quarter, I brought my gun to my cheek, I focused the top of the coin, I fired the shot, and, by golly, I hit it. Lucky went over about 10 feet to pick it up and I couldn't believe my eyes. I hit the mark on the quarter. Lucky threw the quarter three more times and I hit the mark two times and just touched it with the third shot fired. When a coin is thrown spinning, it's impossible to see the mark, and I said so. Lucky laughed and said, "I know you can't see the mark, but your mind's eye can!"

We all know it takes a split second of time to pull the trigger, the shot has to travel down the barrel and fly to the target. So how does the subconscious mind know when to pull the trigger so the shot arrives at a mark on a spinning target a variable distance away? Don't ask me, but it all happened a long time ago.

# The Gregg Method of Fire Control

A TRAINING
MANUAL
ON POINT
SHOOTING
**HANDGUNS**

## 78 + THE GREGG METHOD OF FIRE CONTROL

*Fig. 30. U.S. Border Patrol Agent, San Ysidro, CA*

In 1985 I was training at the Border Patrol Range East of San Ysidro, California and the shooters were shooting very well. While working with this particular shooter I began to get vibrations from my subconscious about an experience I had back in 1973 when I first discovered where accuracy came from in point-shooting.

Recalling this, I looked right into the eyes of the shooter and told him what I believed was the answer to perfect shooting. We then set the handgun to our point of concentration, and the shooter fired one, two, three, four and five rounds of .38 caliber semi-wadcutter ammunition and I looked to see the smallest group I had ever seen.

## Beginning to be a Point-Shooter with the Handgun

In 1969, as manager of the Seattle Gun Club, I began to teach what was then commonly referred to as "Instinctive Shooting".

At first I ran into real problems in teaching some people how to shoot a washer out of the air with a BB gun. It was not a difficult feat, but some people had an awful time learning to do it. Through trial and error, I found that in almost all cases their inability to shoot straight was related to either their eye system, the fit of the gun, and in some cases looking at the end of the gun instead of the target.

My initial experience into the world of point or instinctive* shooting proved to me that with very few repetitions, a person with hardly any skill could become very highly skilled in a very short period of time if they had the correct training.

One night while watching Gun Smoke, one of my favorite programs on TV, Matt Dillon got into a gunfight out in front of the Longbranch Saloon. It was a standoff between Matt and a real bad hombre. When the bad guy went for his gun, quick as lighting Matt drew and shot the poor fellow stone dead with a single shot. It was just great how the good guy always seems to win. It got me to thinking about why one shooter is so much better than another. I knew Matt had to be doing something the other fellow wasn't and I thought I could figure out what. I knew Matt Dillon was confident, fearless, he was brave, and he knew how to shoot straight.

Based on this belief and my experiences while teaching shotgun shooting, I bought my first handgun in 1971. It was a Model 28 Smith & Wesson 357 Magnum that would handle .38's. I bought a case of wadcutters from a friend of mine and along with some bobber targets** set out to learn to shoot as good at a standing target as the greatest of the great, Ed McGivern.

---

*There is a general feeling that certain people are born with the instinct to shoot, and I have never believed that. I believe we drive a car instinctively, we ride a bicycle instinctively, and we can do anything instinctively, or subconsciously after we learn how.
** A bobber target is an upper-body profile made of stiff cardboard. A paper target overlay is attached to shoot at.

I did not know how to hold the revolver, so I got the grip from Bill Jordon's book, "No Second Place Winner". I did not know exactly how to pull the trigger, but it had to be smooth, as the shots had to be very accurate. I practiced for a short time with a penny on the rib of the gun until the penny would stay in place from start to finish. I also learned that the stronger I held the gun, the steadier the penny became and the less vibrations I would send to the end of the barrel.

I learned to hold my arms at the most natural pointing isosceles position at chest height as I knew I would have more strength in controlling the recoil, especially with two hands on the gun and it is a natural pointing position. I never thought of breath control at the time and it was just as well as it was not important. I later figured out that the system doesn't naturally breath during the critical period of time the weapon is firing.

When I began giving shotgun lessons with an air rifle, the targets were hand made aluminum washers. The starting target was 3½″ in diameter, so I went to a stationery store and bought a sheet of fluorescent paper. Back at home I cut a 3½″ circle out of the sheet of fluorescent paper. The next target I used in teaching shotgun shooting via an air rifle was 2½″ in diameter, so I cut a 2½ circle out of the sheet of fluorescent paper. The last target I would sometimes give a shooter would be a nickel or a dime, so I cut a ¼″ square out of the sheet of fluorescent paper. (Squares are easier to cut than circles). On the first bobber target, I placed the 3½″ circle in the center of the chest. On the second target I placed the 2½″ circle in the center of the chest and on the third target I placed the ¼″ square in the center of the chest.

With all my ideas in order, I gathered up my handgun, three bobber targets, a hammer, three nails and 50 rounds of .38 Caliber Wadcutter Ammunition. At the Seattle Gun Club, I had just a short journey to an old logging road that provided a safe place to shoot a handgun with lots of large Douglas fir trees for a backstop. When I left home with all my supplies I figured that if I didn't learn something after firing 50 rounds of ammunition, it would be time to go home.

I went down the logging road and stopped at the first Douglas fir tree to which I nailed the bobber target with the 3½″ circle on it. I then paced off a shooting distance of 15 feet, as the greatest of all pistol shooters Ed McGivern had shot 5 out of 6 shots into a playing card size group in two-fifths of a second at a distance of 15 feet. At this time I was not interested in the speed of fire, I just wanted to know where accuracy in pointing the handgun came from.

I loaded five rounds into my new handgun so I could get 10 repetitions per box of 50. With my two handed grip I set the handgun at chest level and pointed it at the 3½″ circle on the target and began to fire one, two, three, four and five shots. The size of the cone of fire was about 14″ in diameter, not good. I reloaded and again pointed the handgun at my point of concentration and fired again and again and very shortly my box of 50 rounds was gone, the dimension of the cone of fire stayed about the same each time I shot and I really don't think I learned anything.

Early in the morning of the second day I left home with another 50 rounds of ammunition and headed down the logging road for my shooting area. On the way I thought about the first day of shooting and decided to hang the second bobber target with the 2½″ circle of fluorescent paper in the center of the chest area and then I paced off a distance of 15 feet. I loaded my handgun, pointed it at the smaller mark on the target and fired five rounds and immediately I had a change in the dimension of the cone of fire, it was smaller than it was the first day of shooting.

I reloaded and again pointed my handgun at the 2½″ mark on the target and fired again and again, the dimension of the cone of fire remained about the same and very quickly I again ran out of ammunition. I then went home, knowing that by changing the way I saw a target, I reduced the dimension of the cone of bullets fired and I became more skilled than when I began my study only a day ago.

Early in the morning of the third day of shooting I hung the bobber target up with the ¼″ fluorescent mark on it and paced off a distance of 15 feet. I loaded my handgun with five rounds of .38 wadcutters, brought my ¼″ mark into focus, set the handgun to the mark and began to fire one, two, three, four and five rounds and the dimension of the cone of fire, about 6″, was a lot smaller than I had shot before. I reloaded and continued to methodically fire five rounds at a time until 50 rounds were gone. My cone of fire stayed at about 6″, a far cry from what Ed McGivern could shoot. I then began to think that maybe the key to being such a great shot had to lie in how McGivern saw his targets. Was he looking at the target or like shooting the air rifle at the metal washers, was he looking at a point on his targets?

Early in the morning of the fourth day of my study, I left home with another box of 50 rounds of ammunition and down the old logging road I went. When I got to my shooting site, I patched up the holes in the target with the ¼" mark on it, went to my shooting position, loaded my handgun, focused the mark, set the gun to the mark and fired five rounds and the shots showed nothing new from the day before, another 6" group. I reloaded and fired another five rounds and the cone of fire stayed the same.

I then began walking towards the target to cover the holes and suddenly I began to get a feedback from my subconscious that something was happening that shouldn't be. I looked at the target for about five seconds and suddenly realized that when I finished shooting I was not looking at my original focal point, I had to be chasing the bullets as they impacted the target. Excitedly, I thought this could be my problem. I again reloaded and before I proceeded to shoot, I told myself that from the time I begin to fire until I'm finished shooting, I must not let my focal point shift off the mark. I then set the handgun to the mark and fired five rounds, my point of concentration stayed on the mark and the bullets hit touching. I reloaded again, told myself what I was going to do and fired another five rounds and all but one hit touching. A funny thing happened though, I knew before the last bullet left the gun that it was not going to be in perfect control.

THE MIND CONTROLS THE EYE,
THE EYE CONTROLS THE HAND,
THE HAND CONTROLS THE GUN
AND THE GUN CONTROLS THE BULLETS.
THE STEADIER THE EYE, THE STEADIER THE BULLETS.

## The Eye System

If you listed all the requirements for a skilled shooter none of them would be more important than understanding the eye system and its relationship to shooting straight.

Everyone has a hero, and one of mine is "Doc" W.F. Carver. He lived during the days of Buffalo Bill. He was called "The Spirit Gun of the West", he was a World Champion Rifle Shot. Several years ago in the Buffalo Bill Museum in Cody, Wyoming I saw his famous saddle adorned with silver dollars, each with a hole in it. On the front of the case holding the saddle was a small card with the notation: "**Over 100 silver dollars attached to this saddle were thrown in the air by noblemen of Europe and other world countries and shot thru by "Doc" Carver with his Winchester 1886 while riding horseback at full speed**". Dr. W.F. Carver was a Nebraska dentist noted for his sharpshooting. In 1883 he was Buffalo Bills partner for the first season of the Wild West Show.

My long gone hero had to have three things to perform his famous shooting act: He had to have a gun that would shoot where he pointed it, he had to have great powers of concentration and he had to have a horse that could run like hell.

In teaching point-shooting I always say the eyes will control how the bullets impact the target, and the fit of the gun will determine where the bullets strike.

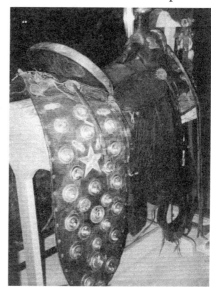

*Fig. 31. "Doc" Carvers Saddle*

## Eye Combinations

Listed below are 14 eye combinations I have found in people over the past 33 years. Eye combinations relate to how people see with both eyes open and account for why so many shooters have the problem of shooting to the left or right of a point or concentration in point-shooting both handguns and shotguns, while shooting with both eyes open. The size of this sample represents eye combinations of 2870 students.

### Percent of Sample

1. Right Handed/Right Master Eye ............................49.0%
2. Right Handed/ 50X50 Vision ...............................15.4%
3. Right Handed/Left Master Eye.............................11.5%
4. Right Handed/Right Dominant Eye .........................8.4%
5. Right Handed/Left Dominant Eye ..........................4.0%
6. Left Handed/Left Master Eye..............................3.1%
7. Right Handed/Right Master Eye (Unstable) ................2.0%
8. Left Handed/50/50 Vision .................................1.3%
9. Left Handed/Right Master Eye.............................1.2%
10. Left Handed/Left Dominant Eye ..........................0.5%
11. Left Handed/Right Dominant Eye .........................0.4%
12. Right Handed/Left Master Eye (Unstable) ................0.2%
13. Double Cross Dominant ..................................1.1%
14. Parallel Dominant ......................................1.8%

## Master Eye

Most shooters have heard of what is commonly called a master eye. I've defined it as one that exists when all objects seen with both eyes open, lie at a right angle to either the right or left eye. The pupil of this particular eye would then be the origin of a controlling line of sight, and the eye power difference between the two eyes would be 20%. Using a factor of 100, if the right eye is a master eye, the right eye would control 60% of a persons total vision and the left eye 40% for a total of 100% vision.

 **1. Right Master Eye** (R 60x40) 49% of sample

*Fig. 32. This agent is right handed with a master right eye. This combination of eyes and hands was found in 49% of a sampling of 2870 people*

A person with a master right eye or master left eye on the same side as the master hand has the option of shooting with both eyes open, or they have the option of closing the opposite eye while they shoot. Most everyone who has a master eye on the same side as the master hand and even those people who do not have a master eye prefer or would like to point handguns with both eyes open as the act of pointing is a natural function.

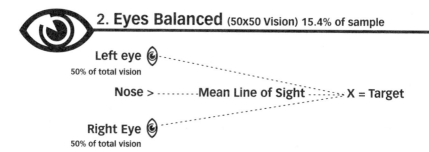

## 2. Eyes Balanced (50x50 Vision) 15.4% of sample

Left eye
50% of total vision

Nose > ········Mean Line of Sight ······> X = Target

Right Eye
50% of total vision

*Fig. 33. Right Handed, Eyes Balanced —50 X 50 Vision*

A 50 X 50 person has three lines of sight: one from the right eye, one from the left eye and a controlling line of sight half way between the eyes.

This combination is the second most frequently found. If a 50/50 person puts a pen in the right or left hand and points it at my eye, I look back through the pen and see the controlling line of sight possibly moving a little to the left or right of the nose or it could be stationary at a point in the immediate area of the nose. These people see with an equal amount of vision in both eyes, everything they see will lie at a right angle to a stationary or variable

Fig. 34. A 50 X 50 right or left handed shooter would be pointing any handgun very similar to the position shown in Fig. 34. A gun fits if it supports the controlling ling of sight that's looking where you want the shot to go. The controlling line of sight lies halfway between the eyes.

point halfway between the eyes. This point would then be the origin of a mean or average line of sight. In shooting the handgun, as long as the barrel is held well below eye level, it would not tend to shoot to the left for a right-handed shooter, or to the right for a left handed shooter. In firing the handgun without training, these people have a 50/50 chance of cross firing with the handgun with both eyes open. The instinct to point has the ability to over ride the unstable controlling line of sight.

## 3. Right Handed/Left Master Eye 11.5% of sample

Shooters who fall into this category of eyes and hands have the highest probability of cross firing or shooting to the left of a point of concentration in pointing the handgun. Right or left master eyed shooters do not like to shoot with the weak eye to make the gun fit simply because they don't see as well.

*Fig. 35. This agent is cross dominant—pistol carried on the right side with a left master eye.*

There are several things that can be done to correct the problem of cross firing:

**Solution #1:** We could shut the strong eye and shoot with the weak eye.

**Solution #2:** We could take the gun and holster to the weak side. The only problem with this solution is the older we get the harder it is to make the change from the strong to the weak side. In the years I've trained law enforcement I think I've only had a half dozen shooters complete the change from the strong to the weak side in handgun shooting.

**Solution #3:** Anything you point is always out of focus. The instinct to point has the ability to override the influence of the opposite strong eye. *If the 3rd method of eliminating cross firing fails, go to solution #4.*

**Solution #4:** Statistics tell us that, 70% of the time, if a person gets into a confrontation, it will happen within 5 to 10 feet from the bad guy who generally shoots, first. If I did not know if I were cross dominant, I could take a pencil hold it vertically in the right hand, arm extended and with both eyes open, point the pencil at a spot on a wall them immediately close the right eye and if the pencil is right on what you pointed it at, then you, by my definition, you would be cross dominant. *(See Checking The Eye System—Page 103)*

**Solution #5:** One of the ways I now use in training cross dominant shooters is to put the handgun in the strong right hand and cast it off to support the opposite controlling line of sight. It is a very good way to solve a problem of cross firing and it can be done with little practice at the range or in the confines of your own home while dry firing and checking to see if the weapon supports the controlling line of sight no matter its origin.

In the beginning of firearms training it would be invaluable to know how each person in a class sees so if they are right handed and left eyed or left handed and right eyed, students from the beginning of training should be taught to shoot on the same side as the master eye. The right or wrong of what we say or do in either right or wrong based on the end result!

## Cross Dominant Shooter

Fig. 36. Right Handed/Left Master eyed shooter casting his weapon off to support the left master eye

To cast the weapon from the right to the left side to support the left controlling eye: Simply draw the weapon from the holster, break the right grip to the right to cast the handgun **off** to the left until the barrel supports the controlling line of sight.

Left handed/right master eyed shooters would do the reverse. Any time you move the weapon from the left to the right you cast it **on** to support a controlling line of sight.

Years ago I had a student who had a master left eye and he was right handed. For 19 years he barely qualified at the range. He did not want to shut his strong eye to shoot, and he did not want to change the handgun to the left hand so he continued to cross fire all those years to the left of his intended point of impact when qualifying.

Before I met this officer I was advised of his qualifying problem and was asked if I could I find the problem and perhaps fix it. During the orientation I checked his eyes and he was left master eyed and right handed and he wore his holster on his right side. I asked him if he had any problems qualifying and he admitted that generally he did.

When he got to the range and when his turn to shoot came up I took his handgun, loaded it with 5 rounds of .38 wadcutters gave him the weapon, he put it in his right hand, he set the handgun to the intended point of impact, I set my hand to his in this initial hands-on phase of training. I told him to fire one, two, three, four and five shots and as expected all the shots went a foot to the left at a distance of 15 feet. I reloaded the handgun, gave it to the shooter he set the gun to where we wanted the shots to go, I set my hand to his and told him to fire and he fired 5 rounds and as expected all shots went a foot to the left of the intended point of impact.

We then continued to repeat the same sequence, 50 shots fired in 10 repetitions and they all went a foot to the left of our point of concentration. I then told him that I couldn't handle his shooting to the left for two days in a row and that I was going to do something about it. The next time his turn to shoot came up I told him to put the handgun in his left hand and he resisted, he didn't like the feel of the handgun in the left hand so I told him to do it anyway. We then set the handgun to where I wanted the bullets to go, the shooter fired five rounds and they were in a 8″ group around our point of concentration. Not good shooting, but with his mind mostly on the gun being in the left hand, his shooting was not that bad. I repeated this same sequence with the handgun in the left hand and after three or so repetitions his overall group began to tighten. I then told him that I was happy with his progress and that changing the handgun to the left hand is not easy but he was doing a great job, he gave me a dirty look and said nothing. We finished the second box if ammunition and I wondered what the third box of ammunition would do to his learning curve. When we began to shoot the third box of ammunition, I could see the cone of fire get much tighter to about a 5″ group and after firing a total of 150 rounds I could see he was spending less time worrying about the handgun being in the left hand and more time concentrating on where he wanted the shots to go and the class ended the first day of training. I then told my problem shooter to bring a left handed holster for the second day of shooting and he gave me another dirty look!

The second and last day of training I always check the retention of each student and it should be 100%. They should shoot just as good in the beginning of the second day as they were shooting at the end of the first day of training. My initial concern the second day of training is in the fit of the handgun and the possibility of shooting low. After checking the fit for each person, we began "Walk and Draws" and my cross-dominant shooter did really well. For most of the daylight the second day we continued "Walk and Draws" and learning to shoot from whatever position the officer could be in at the time the weapon is needed.

Back at the range for night shooting and an hour and half later it's all over. I then cornered my cross-dominant student and told him I was really proud of his shooting. He did very well. A month later the officer in charge of training called me and said they were qualifying everyone in the department and when that particular cross-dominant person finished shooting he shot the same score as he had always shot with the handgun in the right hand, not good. The colonel then told me that he gathered up an instructor and sent the problem shooter back to the range to shoot for a qualifying score with the handgun in the left hand. When the smoke cleared the cross-dominant shooter had shot the highest score since joining the police department 19 years earlier but I'll bet he still didn't like shooting with the gun in this left hand.

+ + +

My average class size is 10 students, each student shoots an average of 150 rounds the first day, so in watching 1500 rounds of ammunition impact a single steel target and listening to my critique, a lot is learned about point shooting by officers who probably never had pointed a handgun before with any kind of accuracy. Most generally 85% of a class makes the Hole in One Club during the initial 150 rounds fired the first day of training. In order to join the "Hole In One Club" the shooter must shoot five bullets touching at a distance of 15 feet from the steel target.

I call it monkey see, monkey do! There's a lot of cybernetics involved in learning to point shoot in a class of 5 to 10 shooters. Firing a gun only substantiates a mental process, so the key to being a great shot lies in the mental process, which I have always believed is 95% of shooting straight. I believe that when the shooter is stacking the bullets into the same hole, I believe their level of concentration is 99.9%.

## 4. Right Handed/Right Dominant Eye 8.4% of sample

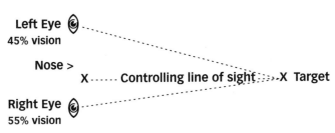

With both eyes open, a dominant right eyed person has 100% vision but the difference in vision power between the eyes is 10%. The right eye is 10% stronger than the left. The right eye has 55% of total eye power and the left would have 45% for a total of 100% vision.

The handgun will fit if it supports the controlling line of sight lying halfway between the right eye and the center of the nose.

A right handed/right dominant eyed person should have a little concern about the possibility of cross firing to the left of their point of concentration but probability is low as the controlling line of sight is only 25% of the pupilary distance to the left eye. Dominant eyed shooters have half the probability of shooting to the left as a 50 X 50 person in shooting handguns. The problem of cross firing for these people is rare because the handgun is held well below the controlling line of sight. In shooting the shotgun I always have these people shut the opposite eye as shooting to the left becomes probable with the much longer barreled shotgun.

##  5. Right Handed/Left Dominant Eye 4.0% of sample

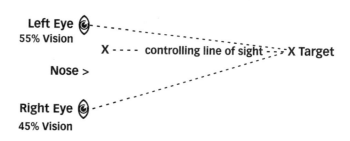

The right handed left dominant eyed person is almost as cross dominant as the right handed left master eyed person. All of these people, when shooting with sights, prefer to close the right eye and cast their head to the right (Cast On) to shoot with the strongest eye. They have a 75% probability of cross firing when pointing the gun in the right hand, shooting with both eyes open.

Cross firing is always probable because the instinct to point has the ability to over ride the influence of the strong left eye. These shooters prefer to shoot with the handgun in the strong hand and could close the strong eye to prevent cross firing if it continues to happen. Another option would be to cast the weapon to the left (Cast Off) to support the controlling line of sight, which would lay half way between the nose and the left eye.

##  6. Left Handed/Left Master Eye 3.1% of sample

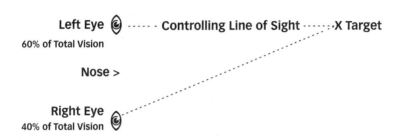

Fig. 37. Left Handed/Left Master Eye

This is the most frequent hand/eye combination found in left-handed people. Only 89 people out of 2870 sampled fell into this category. People who see in this manner naturally prefer to shoot with both eyes open.

A left master eye exists when all objects seen with both eyes open lie at a right angle to the pupil of the left eye. The pupil of the left eye is then the origin of the controlling line of sight and the power difference between the two eyes would be 20%. 60% of the total eye power would lie with the left eye, and 40% of total eye power would lie with the right eye.

## 7. Right Handed/Right Master Eye (Unstable) 2% of sample

This condition exists when the controlling line of sight originates at a point other than the center of the right eye, then the right eye takes over and the controlling line of sight moves to the pupil of the right eye. If I repeat the eye test multiple times the same eye sequence happens. I have always called this movement "Instability". I have never seen this condition affect a handgun shooter and their ability to shoot straight as the weapon is normally out of focus well below the controlling line of sight.

Instability affects shotgun shooting in that the end of the barrel does not want to be steady to the target at the time shots are fired. To correct the problem, I'll have the shooter close the opposite eye as the stock is placed to the face then, the barrel will be steady to the target at the time shots are fired.

 ## 8. Left Handed (50x50) Vision 1.2% of sample

In sight shooting, handgun shooters who fall into this hand/eye combination have always shut the opposite right eye when using sights. In pointing the handgun with both eyes open they have a 50/50 chance of cross firing to the right of a point of concentration. In training I always have them begin shooting with both eyes open. If after 50 to 100 rounds of fire and cross firing continues, I would have the shooter shut the right eye during the time the weapon is firing. Most generally, however, for a person with 50 X 50 vision, it isn't long before the pointed handgun moves totally out of focus and the possibility of shooting to the right becomes remote. No matter what the eye combination, it is more natural for the shooter to shoot with both eyes open but a very small number of people just can't do it.

## 9. Left Handed/Right Master Eye 1.2% of sample

Left handed shooters who have a master right eye have the highest probability of shooting to the right of a point of concentration than any other hand/eye combination for a left handed person. People with this eye/hand combination normally sight shoot with the weapon in the strong left hand and cast the head and right eye to the left for sight alignment. In point shooting we should properly bring the gun to support the controlling line of sight one way or another. There are options cross dominant people have to make the gun fit.

**Option #1:** Before I tried any of the below solutions to cross firing, I would first rely on the instinct to point to override the influence of the right master eye. I would have the shooter shoot at least 100 rounds of fire before trying a method of correcting a problem. Beginning point shooters sometimes have the habit of looking down at the handgun instead of concentrating on where they want the shot/s to go. Looking down at the handgun will tell you nothing about where shots will go and being a master right eyed shooter the gun will never look right until the end of the gun touches the right eyes line of sight then if shots are fired, they will all go to the right of where the shooter wants them to go.

The habit of looking down at the handgun is not hard to break and once it is broken, the weapon moves out of focus, concentration to the point of impact becomes improved and hopefully, cross firing to the right ceases.

**Option #2:** In shooting the handgun, I some times encourage the younger shooter to go find or buy a right-handed holster and switch all shooting to the right side. This change should be done at the academy level. It takes repetitions and it can be done as quickly as over night. When the transition begins, everything will feel "funny" to the shooter but the more we use the new gun hand the less "funny" it will feel and when we finish the transition, the gun in the weak hand shouldn't feel funny at all. It should feel natural and at this point it will be instinctive. A gun fits if it supports the line of sight that's looking where you want the bullets to go.

**Option #3:** The left handed/right master eyed shooter can draw and cast the weapon to the right to support the right master eye. Casting the pistol to support the controlling line of sight can be most natural and the change to this method of shooting can be done with few repetitions and it can be easier than changing the weapon to the opposite right hand. I would suggest the problem shooter put the handgun in the left hand and cast it to support the right eye and then check the sights and they should be supporting the line of sight that's looking at where the shooter wants the shot/s to go. In repeating this exercise you would be developing "muscle memory" and after so many repetitions the weapon should instinctively move to this newly programmed position, then, move the handgun down and away from the line of sight until you don't see it anymore, all you see is the point of impact while shooting.

 **10. Left Handed/Left Dominant Eye** 0.5% of sample

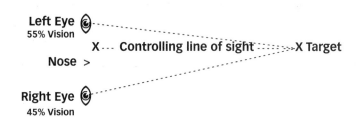

With both eyes open a dominant eyed person has 100% vision but the difference in vision power between the two eyes is 10%. The left eye is 10% stronger than the right eye. The left eye has 55% of total eye power and the right has 45%.

The left handed/left dominant eyed person should have some concern about the possibility of cross firing to the right of a point of concentration in shooting the handgun. In shooting the shotgun I have these left- handed people shut the opposite eye, which totally eliminates the probability of shooting to the right.

##  11. Left Handed/Right Dominant Eye 0.4% of sample

Cross firing is always probable because the instinct to point has the ability to over ride the influence of the strong eye. The very few people having this eye combination prefer to shoot with the handgun in the left hand and if cross firing does occur, they could close the strong eye to solve the problem or better yet, do as the above shooter has done.

*Fig. 38. The left handed/right dominant eyed person is as cross dominant as the right handed/left dominant eyed person. Each category of eyes and hands have a 75% probability if cross firing in pointing the handgun. The above shooter has cast his pistol "on" to support his controlling line of sight located halfway between the nose and the right eye.*

## 12. Right Handed/Left Master Eye (Unstable) 0.2% of sample

With a pointer pen or pencil in the right hand the controlling line of sight begins at a point somewhere between the left eye and the nose then the left eye takes over and pulls the line of sight to the center of the left pupil.

This person has the following options:

1. Shoot with the left eye closed.

2. Change the handgun to the left side.

3. Keep the handgun on the right side and fire 20 repetitions of 5 rounds per repetition and see if the instinct to point has the ability to override the influence of the strong left eye to pull the weapon and bullets to the left of a point of concentration.

 ## 13. Double Cross Dominant 1.1% of sample

This combination of eyes and hands is one of the two most unusual combinations I've found. If I put a pen in a double cross dominant persons right hand and have them raise it to my master right eye, I then look back through the pen and see it in line with the checkee's* left eye. If I put the pen in the checkee's left hand and have them point it at my right eye then I'll see it in line with the checkee's right eye. If I have the checkee put both hands down at their sides, I then reverse the test by holding the pen in my right hand and point it at the checkee's right eye and the checkee will see it in line with my right eye. I then have the checkee raise his right hand and arm above an angle of 45 degrees and they will feel a change in eye power from the right to the left eye, I then point the pen at the checkee's left eye and they will see it in line with my right eye. Raising a hand and arm

---

*Checkee*—Person being checked. *Checker*—Person doing the checking.

above an angle of 45 degrees can change some master right eyed people to a left master eyed person. If these people pointed the handgun at a target with the gun in the right hand, both eyes open, they would have a very high probability of shooting to the left of a point of concentration.

If the same shooter held the handgun in the left hand they would have a very high probability of shooting to the right of a point of concentration, so, no matter what they do, it would be wrong to shoot with both eyes open. This person was wired by a non-union man!

## 14. Parallel Dominant 1.8% of sample

Having this combination of eyes and hands would allow these shooters to shoot from either the right or left side with both eyes open. If the gun were put in the right hand and the right arm raised to a firing position, the right eye is the normal master eye. If the handgun were put in the left hand and raised to a firing position, the left eye becomes a master eye. I have found the "trigger" to this particular combination to lie in the opposite arm when raised above an angle of 45 degrees. These people will feel eye strength increase as the weapon is changed from the right to the left hand as it is raised to a firing position. I have not found a left handed parallel dominant person.

## Another Exotic Eye Combination

A right handed/right master eyed person puts a pen vertically in their right hand and points it at my right eye. I look back and see the pen in line with the checkee's right eye. I then have the checkee put the pen in the left hand and line it up to my right eye. I then look to see the pointer in line with the checkee's nose. The eyes became balanced in vision power upon changing the pointer to the left hand. I was very curious about when the change took place so I had this particular officer extend both arms out in front of him with the pointer in the right hand and point it at my right eye and it was lined up with his right eye. With the arms still extended, I had the checkee transfer the pointer to his left hand and immediately his eyes became equal in vision power (50 X 50) and the pointer lined up with the officer's nose. This particular shooter should shoot with both eyes open. It is most natural with the handgun in the right hand. With the handgun in the left hand the shooter would have a 50 X 50 probability of cross firing to the right of a point of concentration correctable by closing the right eye. As a final check I had the checkee put both hands on the pointer and again point it at my right eye. I then looked to see it in line with the checkee's right eye. Shooting with both hands on the handgun, both eyes open, did not present a problem for this particular shooter. With the handgun in the left hand the instinct to point has the ability to over ride the influence of the right eye so if the shooter had the weapon in the left hand, they still have the ability to shoot straight with both eyes open. I have never found anyone that could explain this phenomenon.

## Checking the Eye System

The checkee should take a pen or pencil and hold it with first the strong hand and then the support hand at arms length with the points of the pen or pencil held vertically upwards. If the checker does not know how they see, it is best if the checker does the checking with the weak eye closed.

With both eyes open, the checkee should point the pen or pencil at the checkers remaining eye. The checker at this point can easily see where the pencil is lined up, relative to the eyes of the checkee. It is important to classify the eyes when the pointer first comes to the face. If the pointed object is lined to the center of the right eye, they have a master right eye. If the pointed object is lined to a point half way between the right eye and the nose, the checkee has a dominant right eye. If the pointed object lines up to the nose, the checkee has 50 X 50 vision in that one eye has the same amount of strength as the other and neither eye is dominant or master over the other. If the pointed object lines up halfway between the left eye and the nose, the checkee has a dominant left eye and if the pointed object lines up to the left eye, the checkee has a master left eye.

It is very important to identify a shooters eye system. Only master right eyed, right handed people or left eyed, left handed people have the option of shooting the shotgun with both eyes open or one eye closed. It is more natural for people to learn point shooting the handgun with both eyes open regardless of the shooters eye combination.

*Fig. 39. The "Checkee" with a 50x50 Eye Combination*

# Problems in Shooting Straight

## Shooting High

Shooting high is not a common error in point shooting and is mainly due to looking down at the handgun or the front sight. It's subconscious and understandable after so many years of looking at the end of the handgun. Looking down at the handgun, held at chest level will tell you nothing about where fired bullets will go. If the barrel of the pistol is off the mark just an $1/8^{th}$ of and inch at a distance of 15 feet the error of the shot with a 4˝ barreled handgun will be 5.6˝.

**Using the formula:**

$$\frac{\text{Length of the Barrel}}{\text{Error of the Barrel}} = \frac{(\text{Distance to the target}) \times (12)}{\text{Error of the Bullet}}$$

$$\frac{4}{.125} \times \frac{(15)(12)}{X} \qquad X = 5.6˝ = \text{Error of the bullet}$$

## Shooting Low

I have found the main reason for shooting low is due to a bent wrist. We get it by bringing the handgun to eye level in sighting during the learn to shoot process and after so many repetitions it becomes subconscious for the wrist to be bent. It will stay in this bent condition for both sighting and pointing the handgun. In a shooting to live situation, in which the officer doesn't have time or light to sight a gun, the results could be disastrous for the officer.

The second reason for shooting low is due to a conscious thought process during the time shots are fired, so even if your handgun fits perfect, you can still shoot low. Thinking dilates the eyes and terminates our hearing (ask my wife). Thought during the period of time the weapon is discharging is out of a proper shooting sequence, as conscious thought needs only to be used to learn.

## Shooting Low-Fit or Focus

If a shooter has a problem of shooting low and doesn't know the origin of the error it can be found by saying "Is it fit or is it my focus, am I looking at the whole target or am I looking where I want the shot/s to go?"

First, check the focus of the eye by doing a walk and draw. Walk, stop, identify the target, draw the handgun, focus the mark, then focus the top of the mark and fire one round.

If the shot is on the money, the problem is solved, by focusing to a higher level of concentration. If the initial shot consistently goes more than 2″ low at a training distance of 15 feet, the problem is fit and reprogramming is necessary. *(See Programming the Fit and Reprogramming the Subconscious. Page 123)*

## The Dishonest Shooter

Those new to point-shooting without instruction, are most apt to set the handgun to chest level in a modified isosceles stance and then look down at the gun and it will look like it is going to shoot low because the weapon is low relative to the eye system. At this point they will likely make a correction to the end of the barrel, fire the first shot, it will likely go high. So they make another correction to lower the next shot and continue this pattern until the gun is empty of ammunition. Moving the barrel up and down to correct a point of impact is likely to show a large cone of fire after all shots have been fired and I would classify the shooter as "dishonest".

## The Honest Shooter

If the same shooter were honest, with the weapon held at chest level, and fired one, two, three, four and five shots without any correction to the end of the barrel, all shots may go low, the dimension of the cone of fire would be equal to the total deviation of the shooters point of concentration.

To critique the shooter, I would say the shooter is honest. If the cone of fire is very small, they would be highly skilled but, the gun doesn't fit.

## Right Handed/Right Master Eyed Shooter Shooting to the Right of a Point of Concentration— Gun Hand Too Small for the Grip on the Handgun

I have seldom seen a right-handed shooter shoot to the right of a point of concentration but it can happen and it happens to people with small hands. Most of these people have been females, only one male shooter has fallen into this category of shooter.

It is impossible to buy a handgun that will fit comfortably in the hands of all people, so your department or service, hopefully buys a handgun that will fit the hand of the greater percentage of people. In placing the pistol in the normal size hand, the first joint of the trigger finger should be placed on the trigger to avoid take-up. Where the trigger could be placed on the finger is optional for the smaller than average handed person.

In shooting a standard size handgun made for the average person, the smaller handed person will find it near impossible to set the trigger to the proper position (first joint) on the trigger finger. If, however, the short fingered person cast the grip in the hand to the left, moving the barrel to the right to reach the "proper" position for the trigger finger, then subsequent shots fired will tend to impact to the right of a point of concentration. If the shooter then straightens the weapon in the hand, the trigger likely ends up on the forward pad of the trigger finger. At this point the best thing to do is shoot a few rounds and see what happens. If the shot is on the money, then shooting with the trigger on the forward pad is right. It's not standard but it's correct based on the end result.

Years ago I had a lady student who set her handgun to the target and pulled the trigger with the forward pads of both trigger fingers. It was awhile before I noticed what she was doing but when I asked her about what she was doing she explained she had more strength to pull the trigger with the tips of two fingers than if she used just one. It makes perfect sense for a small-handed person to improvise when smaller guns are unavailable. We should do what ever we have to do to make the handgun fit, then skill with the handgun will come.

## A Right Handed Shooter Shooting to the Left or a Left Handed Shooter to the Right

This is due to the lack of a master eye on the same side as the master hand. Several years ago, I had a shooting school in White Horse, Yukon Territories. During the two-hour orientation I check each persons eyes and found two officers who were right handed and left master eyed. I told them that no one can say they're going to cross fire if they shoot with both eyes open but if they do there are ways to fix the problem.

When we got to the range the first cross dominant officer shot right on the money from the beginning and I was happy with his shooting. The other cross dominant shooter fired 200 rounds to the left of his point of concentration. We corrected the problem by having the shooter find a left handed holster and practice drawing from it periodically from the time he arrived home that day until bedtime and again the following morning. When firing began the second day of shooting, my problem shooter shot straight to the mark and made the Hole in One Club twice.

## Reason #2 for a Right Handed Person to Shoot to the Left of a Point of Concentration—Lack of Fit, Lack of Skill

I had a fellow in a class in Laredo who was shooting so inconsistently. I just couldn't believe it! After he fired the first box of 50 rounds, I got to thinking this person is the first person I've ever seen that cannot be taught to point a handgun accurately.

My shooter shot his bullets all over the target and I didn't know why. I kept thinking about my problem shooter while others were shooting until I got a hunch about what could be the problem. I asked for the shooters pistol, checked to make sure it was empty, checked it the second time and gave it back to the shooter and had him point it at my right eye. I looked to see the barrel supporting the right arm instead of his controlling line of sight. I asked him if he was taught to set the handgun supporting the arm and he said, "Yes". I said, "The pistol should support the arm in single handed point shoulder target shooting but when sight shooting with both hands on the weapon and in point-shooting the barrel should support the controlling line of sight".

It made sense to my problem shooter, it's always made sense to me, we changed the fit of the pistol by casting the wrist off to the left to move the barrel to the right to support his controlling right eye. After several repetitions, I had him point the pistol at my right eye and everything looked just fine. I then took the pistol, loaded a clip with five .40 caliber rounds. We then pointed the pistol at a mark on the greased steel target and fired five rounds right on the money. Before this shooter left for the day he made the "Hole in One Club" twice. Technique used in one method of shooting handguns does not necessarily apply to another method of shooting.

# Strength

There are two degrees of strength:

**Conscious Strength** is normal strength used to properly grip the handgun a little less than full strength to reduce the recoil cycle. Some people have greater normal strength than others. Normal strength can be greatly improved by working the hands with a spring grip tool, play dough, rubber ball etc.

**Subconscious Strength** we all have and I have always deemed it truly great strength. We've heard of the mother who picks up the bumper of a vehicle so another can pull a child out of harms way.

One summer, during World War II, I worked in a Kaiser Shipyard in Tacoma, Washington. One night a worker fell off the dock and landed between the pilings and a Liberty Ship. Another worker saw the accident and put his shoulder against the ship and held it away from the dock until a line could be dropped to the man in trouble. After the man was rescued, the hero released his strength on the ship and it moved back into its resting position. I believe, in a shooting to live situation, subconscious strength on the weapon is most apt to come into play for the more aggressive shooter who knows how to shoot.

## Strength on the Grip

The stronger the grip, the shorter the recoil cycle. The grip should not be 100% of your total normal strength. If the grip were set at 100%, the end of the barrel becomes shaky, back off on the strength until the barrel becomes steady and this will be the grip to use in firing any handgun through the .44 magnum.

## Improperly Gripping the Handgun

Fig. 40. Poor grip on the revolver—The backstrap is a radius of a circle, the lower you place the hand, the lower you move the end of the barrel and the point of impact.

## Properly Gripping the Handgun

Fig. 41. Picture of a good grip. The top of the hand should be even with the hump of the backstrap.

Fig. 42. Picture of a Poor Grip—The support hand supports the grip hand but adds little strength in gripping the pistol to control the recoil cycle.

## Pulling the Revolver Trigger

Learning to pull a trigger steady in not difficult. First, check the cylinder to make sure the weapon is unloaded, spin the cylinder and check it again to make sure the gun is unloaded. Add a .25 cent piece to the rib just behind the front sight, set the grip into the hand, set the support hand, tighten the grip to less than maximum and slowly stroke the trigger back and let the hammer fall. Do the sequence again and again and while you're doing this look at the coin, it should be steady from start to finish. Once the .25 cent piece is steady to the rib you'll know your not sending any vibrations to the end of the barrel. Speed in pulling the trigger is likely to increase in training. As a rule, if you increase speed of fire, you decrease accuracy. The beginning point shooter should first gain accuracy and speed of fire will come with confidence. In firing live ammo, pulling the trigger should be no faster than the time it takes the weapon to return to a steady position. Do not shoot in the recoil cycle.

## Homework

Once pulling the trigger is mastered, take a piece of white card stock, add a ½″ black dot to the center of the card, tack and secure it to a wall at chest level and back away from it 12 to15 feet. From a *modified isosceles stance*, set the handgun, to the black dot and pull the trigger, drop the hammer several times keeping the dot in focus from start to finish. If the dot goes out of focus, you'll know your mind is not on the dot and you're probably thinking about pulling the trigger correctly.

*Fig. 43. Picture of a Good Grip—Pistol, Right Side*

*Fig. 44. Picture of a Good Grip—Pistol, Left Side*

# Pulling a Semi-Auto's Trigger—Double Action Only

Pull a semi-auto's trigger the same way you pull a revolver trigger. Don't pull any trigger too fast and don't shoot in the recoil cycle. If the trigger is pulled too fast, the cone of fire will increase, in which case slow down and the cone of fire will decrease. *Fast is fine—accuracy is final!*

The Beretta DOA, Model 96D, 40 Caliber is the standard weapon in the Border Patrol at this time (May 2003). During the change over from revolvers to the semi-autos, a lot of the agents didn't like the weapon and the long trigger pull because it was different from the revolver they carried for years.

After the Border Patrol changed over to the Beretta's, I headed on down Del Rio way to hold several schools for the BP. On the way down I stopped in to visit with a friend of mine and we talked and talked about this and that and as usual the conversation got around to the Beretta pistols they had to carry. My friend said that he didn't like the blankety-blank new gun and that he wished he could carry his Model 19 Smith. He just couldn't get used to the long trigger pull the Beretta had. I had a lot of shooters firing the gun before that day and they were doing very well with the gun after going through transitional training (2000+ rounds of fire) and now, just as many agents were making the Hole in One Club with the Beretta that had made the club with the Model 19 Smith or the Ruger.

I started shooting at the Del Rio Range a couple of days later with a new class of agents, and my friend showed up for the school. During the first day of training 85 to 100% of the shooters make the Hole in One Club and this day was no different. At the end of the day all the agents but my friend made the club. You can imagine the looks my friend got when he returned to the station after the first day of shooting.

The very next day you can't guess who wanted to shoot first, it was my friend. I loaded the pistol with five rounds of .40 caliber ammo, we set the pistol to the focal point and when the smoke cleared, all the bullets touched. "Yahoo" said I! "Yahoo" said the rest of the shooters. Going back to my camp at the end of the day I wondered if my friend would trade the Beretta for the Model 19 now?

Any time we make a change in anything we do, the learning curve goes down, the cone of fire enlarges and will stay enlarged until the transition is complete between any two weapons. If the new gun fits, the learning curve should then move up to where it was when shooting the original weapon and hopefully, surpass it to a higher level of proficiency. You cannot have your mind on the gun and the point of impact at the same time.

Any time we change weapons, whether it be shotguns or handguns, the new gun will feel funny to all of us. The key to shooting the new weapon is to override the feel funny feedback from the subconscious, forget the feedback, focus the eyes to where you want the bullets to go, maintain perfect mindset and shoot!

## Concentration

A few years ago I was having lunch with Charley Pertle. Charley was stationed at the Border Patrol Station in Las Cruces, New Mexico and shot on the National Border Patrol Pistol Team. At lunch I asked him a question and that was "Charley, do you really focus the front sight on your pistol when shooting?" Charley answered, "Yes, you have to, but I really don't look at the front sight, I look at the corner of the front sight". By doing this Charley would have a higher level of concentration than if he looked at the front sight, When the dimension of the line of sight is reduced to the same size as the focal point of the eye, (A very, very small dot) I believe the factor of concentration becomes 100 percent.

---

In pointing the handgun, if the shooter has perfect mindset during the time the weapon is firing, bullets will touch within 15 feet of the steel training target. The mind controls the eyes, the eyes control the hand, the hand controls the gun and the gun controls the bullets, so, mind control is fire control.

---

I believe that as a standard, shooting is 95% mental and 5% physical. When a shooter, however, is stacking his bullets to the same mark the physical part of shooting becomes overridden by the psychological. Shooters will find themselves in a tunnel of concentration during the time the weapon is firing. The origin of the tunnel will be the origin of the controlling line of sight and the end of the tunnel will be the point of impact. The time it takes to get into and out of the tunnel is controlled by the speed of focus.

The highest level of concentration is not needed in a typical gun fight as the distance to the target will likely be within 15 feet of the officer. Is perfect shooting necessary when firing at a distance of 3 to 21 feet? Not really, but having confidence with the weapon you're carrying and having the ability to shoot skillfully, 24 hours of the day, is a lifetime possession. You've got to win the fight before the gun leaves the holster and you win it with confidence and with confidence the officer is least likely to shoot, in a no shoot situation.

## Arjuna the Archer
*A story sent to me by one of my students, Dave Smith.*

**Jim:** The following story is about a metaphorical character who was featured in the *Gagavad Gita* which is a portion of the *Mahabharata*. Arjuna was the student, who more clearly than any of the others, reflected upon and sought to understand the Way. The *Mahabharata* is an Indian story written somewhere around 300 BC–400 AD. It is the longest epic ever written.

The incident to which we refer took place between Arjuna and his archery instructor. It proceeds as follows:

---

It is a necessary part of the story of Arjuna the archer. His archery teacher, pointing to a model of a vulture, the target being its eye, "What can you see Arjuna, as Arjuna aims his arrow?" "I cannot tell you." Teacher: "Why Arjuna?" "Because all I see is eye." He is the only one of the *Pandavas* (students) that passes the teacher's test.

---

Talk about the concept of direct line of sight from the perfectly positioned gun to the center of the target, which you teach us!

I will say this, as a student of 35 years in the martial arts (of which training in modern weapons is one aspect) that the key to exact placement, in addition to proper delivery of technique, body alignment and a well-tuned weapon, rests ultimately in doing so with the proverbial "empty mind."

To the extent that one can achieve this "still point", in addition to the above-mentioned factors, I believe that one can "drive tacks" with bullet placement.

In "Star Wars", Obi Won said "Turn off the computers, Luke" as he speeds through a hail of rocket fire, to place his payload directly into the core of the enemy spaceship "Planet", destroying it.

It becomes more than letting "The force be with you." You BECOME THE FORCE. You are not only aligned with it, but for an instant you become its delivery spear point, It is "Magic".

I think, Jim, that if I was confronted with an evil Atavar, and had a loved one on the razor's edge or if I sensed beyond doubt that I unavoidably faced a situation where it was "kill or be killed" that I would, for an instant, become that energy stream and drive five rounds into the center of the target, one upon the other. I could only do that if I "died to myself" first. If I could not or did not respond in such a way, then I would at that moment be dead, even if my physical body continued to live years into the future.

You, as one of my foremost teachers, have instilled within me, both in the theory and the practice, the POTENTIAL of being able to do just that. The rest would be up to me, and the great energy stream that is the source of all things.

*Namaste!*
—Dave Smith

## Another Story About Arjuna

Japanese masters of self-defense knew more about Arjuna the archer: Invited to a tournament in which skill in archery was tested by having the archers "aim" at the eye of a painted wooden fish set high on a pole, many contestants were asked by a teacher before they released their arrows, what it was they saw. With one exception, they all answered "a fish". Arjuna replied that he saw only the "eye" of the fish, and as might be expected, he alone hit the target. Shooters must develop the capacity to not only to see the whole but any of its parts.

### Testing Your Level of Concentration

I'll put two marks a distance apart for your observation.

• •

Focus the mark on the left and then the mark on the right, then back to the mark on the left etc. and you'll feel a movement in your eye. What's moving is your focal point, a point of concentration. If you're looking at the mark on the left, the mark on the right will be out of focus. Now let's establish a level of concentration by reducing the distance between the marks. Begin with the top two marks shown on the opposite page. Focus one and then the other and you will feel a movement in your eye as you go from one mark to the other without thinking about what you're doing. Continue this exercise until you reach the very bottom. You should feel movement until you reach the single mark at the bottom at which point you'll probably feel no more movement of your focal point. As you move from the upper set of marks to the lower set and finally to a single mark you will feel a deviation in your point of concentration or focal point. Now with just the single mark, look at the left side and then the right and you may still feel a movement in your eye, if so you're doing great and you can be a great shot because your level of concentration is very high.

In firing the handgun, the dimension of the cone of fire will be equal to the total deviation of your point of concentration on where you want the bullets to go. When your line of sight is reduced to the same dimension as the focal point of the eye, your factor of concentration becomes 100%

Explanation: The dimension of fired bullets, as they appear on a target, will be equal to the total movement of the shooters focal point on the target while in the act of shooting. If there is no movement and the level of concentration is 100% the bullets will impact the same point within 15 feet of the target.

## The Psychological Processes of Consistency

We can tell if the conscious mind of a shooter is working or not working based on how the bullets strike the target. In training we only need to control a function of the conscious mind during the time the weapon is firing, which is perhaps 2 to 3 seconds of time. I call this the "Critical Period of Time". Thinking is used to learn. We want to think about what we want to do and then we do it and we continue this sequence until we reach that point where we don't have to think about it anymore, we just do it.

I had a shooter in Laredo that would fire four bullets touching at a distance of 15 feet and drop the fifth bullet six inches low. I'd reload the pistol, we'd set the weapon to our point of concentration and he'd fire four bullets touching and then drop the last shot about 6 inches low. I said nothing and wondered how long dropping the last shot would continue. I reloaded the third clip into the pistol, we'd set the pistol to where we wanted the shots to go and darned if the shooter didn't shoot another four bullets touching and drop the last shot. After doing this three times I finally told the shooter that I wanted to take his picture for the "Hole in One Club" and that I wanted him to quit thinking about how great he was doing after the fourth shot and fire all 5 shots touching. He smiled and said that was exactly what he was doing and let's do it again. I loaded another 5 rounds of .40 caliber ammunition into the pistol, we set the barrel to our point of concentration and when the smoke cleared, all five bullets were touching. Yahoo!!

# Targets

### The Paper Target

Most law enforcement agencies use paper targets. I taught myself on a paper target with a cardboard back called a "bobber target". One problem in shooting paper is that it doesn't ring. This feedback is very important in shortening the learning curve, but as yet I haven't figured out how to make a paper target ring!

If we set a standard paper target on a frame and look at it, we normally see nothing to focus on except perhaps a number! If the eye doesn't have anything to focus on, the line of sight dilates and skill is lost before the first shot is fired.

At night, we can set a point of concentration by visualizing a point on the target where we want the bullets to go, do the same in the hours of daylight. When firearms training begins, add a half inch black or white mark to the sternum of the paper target then after training is complete, you won't need the mark anymore.

Fig. 45. Picture of a paper target with a lot of focal points. Focus a number, the rest of the numbers are out of focus.

## The Steel Target

Back in the late 1960's Holland and Holland Shooting Schools from England came to the Seattle Gun Club to hold a shooting school once a year. The instructor talked about a shotgun pattern board made of steel plates coated with white wash. After firing at a mark on the target the shooter could see the pattern of a shotgun barrel. After thinking about what the instructor said about coating the plate of steel with white wash. I decided their idea of a coating wasn't really very good because white wash dries and having a coating similar to a primer paint that wouldn't dry would be much better to roll out on a flat plate. I ended up buying a can of light colored wheel bearing grease. For a color I went to a paint store and had a white concentrate added and mixed. On a flat steel plate the colored grease rolled easily with a paint-roller and it worked very well for patterning shotguns.

I began to teach myself how to point handguns in 1971 and it wasn't very long before I thought that if I could shoot a flat plate with shotgun shot, then why couldn't I do it with a handgun bullet. I had a steel target made out of ½″ steel and it was mild in temper. After a couple thousand rounds of fire, it got rough to the touch and I noticed the ricochet line was moving back towards the shooter. After cleaning the target with a grease remover, I could see that the roughness was changing the direction of the flack making my first steel target unsafe.

I began calling steel companies about tempered steel and found two types that might work. One was called AR Plate for Abrasion Resistant and the other type was called T-1. I tried both types of steel and ended up using T-1 for the next several years until Border Patrol Headquarters came to the conclusion that if agents were going to pack the .357 revolver for duty purposes they should train with .357 ammunition instead of wadcutters.

My problems began with the first shot fired. My T-1 steel target just wasn't hard enough to hold up to the impact of the heavier .357 Magnum ammunition. After the first days shooting with these loads, I had to change targets after each class and resurface the worn target with a hand grinder. Shooting the heavier loads also began to loosen some of the revolvers as the average shooter would go thru about 450 rounds during two days of shooting and hands were getting sore. I finally finished my contract and left for home knowing that some guns were tougher than others and learning with the heavier ammunition was a lot more difficult than beginning with lighter loads and finishing up with .357 magnum ammunition.

In January 1998 I heard about another type of steel being used to fabricate targets for silhouette shooting so I had a double-headed target made so I would have four times the target life that I had with a single headed target. Since using ballistic steel targets I've had nothing but admiration for the longevity of a target. Shooting 1500 rounds of .40 caliber ammunition at a 3/8″ thick steel plate will concave the metal so every half day of shooting I turn the target around or swap ends to "pull" the target back to a straight condition. In addition to turning the target every half day, I get out the saw-horses and smooth the target to its original smooth surface condition with a grinder after shooting about 10,000 rounds on a target.

The Double Headed Target I use is 3/8" thick, 15" wide and 35" high.

*Fig. 46. Picture of a Double Headed Target with One Round of Buckshot*

*Fig. 47. Rolling Out the Grease*

I use colored wheel bearing grease to coat my steel targets. I buy a gallon can of light colored grease and take it to a paint store. I then have some one add the color of gold to the grease and mix it until I have gold grease.

With a putty knife, I add enough to the target to get a light coating on the target that will last most of a normal shooting day. At the end of the day, I cover the target with a plastic bag and store it in a secure place along with the front and back target holding stakes.

# Fitting the Handgun to the Shooter

In the Border Patrol, all duty handguns are owned by the government. It isn't possible to physically alter a firearm in any way to make it fit large or small hands of big and small people. It is, however, a common practice to buy an approved pair of grips that can shorten or lengthen the "pull" * to accommodate out of normal size hands.

The final line for the taller or shorter than normal people shooting guns that don't fit them, is to do as good as you can do with what you have to work with.

## PROGRAMMING THE FIT

**Option #1**—From the beginning, every shooter will have an initial "feel" for fit. "Feel" is subconscious feedback and it's right or wrong based on where the first shot strikes. In the beginning of training a class, I'll sometimes have a new student set his loaded handgun to a mark I'll leave on the steel target. I'll then look down at the barrel and generally see it pointing low. I ask the shooter if he's pointing right to the mark, and most generally they will say yes, then I'll quietly say fire and the shot will go maybe a foot low. I'll again have the shooter set the handgun to the mark on the target and I'll again look to see the barrel pointed downward. I'll say fire and the second shot will go low. The shooter's fit is wrong and we both agree we must change the shooters "feel".

### Reprogramming the Subconscious

The feel feedback is subconscious, so we must get into the subconscious and reprogram it. The only way to get into the subconscious is through the conscious. At this point we'll set the handgun to a mark on the target

---

*Length of the pull is the distance between the front, center of the trigger and the center of the backstrap.

for the third time then I'll reset the weapon by changing the angle of the shooters wrist until I see the barrel level. At this point the shooter's "feel" will tell them that they are going to shoot high. I then tell the shooter to fire and the shot generally goes right on or very close to the mark, but to the shooter it felt like they were going to shoot high but it didn't, so we'll repeat the same sequence again. I'll have the shooter point the handgun at the mark, then, I'll reset the weapon until I see the barrel straight and level, I'll have the shooter fire and the shot is likely to go right on. To the shooter, however, it will still "feel" like they are going to shoot high so we continue to repeat the sequence again and about the fourth or fifth repetition of setting, resetting and firing, the shooters "feel" will change but the shooter probably won't know it has changed. I'll have the shooter repeat the sequence again by setting the pistol to the mark then I'll look down and probably see the barrel level.

The shooter, at this point, will likely break the wrist to raise the barrel, I'll look down to see the barrel pointing high and I'll say fire, and the shot will go high and to the shooter it felt like it was going to shoot high before the shot was fired.

At this point I'll have the shooter reload, set the barrel to the mark and fire 5 rounds without any reset or adjustment of the wrist and the first shot is likely to go right on. Once the wrist is reprogrammed it is not likely to change in pointing the handgun. The first shot fired will determine the fit, the rest of the shots will go where the first shot goes if the point of concentration remains steady to the mark. In programming the fit we want the first and remaining shots to feel right and be right to where we want them to go.

**Option #2**—A head start in programming the handgun to fit can be done in the confines of your own home. Take an empty handgun, make sure it is unloaded, and point it at a black mark in the center of a piece of white paper secured to a wall at about chest level. At this point have a second person just look at the handgun from a side view and they should see the barrel level and not pointing downward.

**Option #3**—When I first began to shoot the handgun, I had no previous training in handgun shooting and when I set my gun to a target my wrist was naturally straight. When I began teaching law enforcement, the majority of the shooters set the handgun to the target with a crooked wrist and it's still standard procedure to straighten the wrist to make a barrel level to the mark on a straightaway target.

It wasn't hard to find the origin of the error as in sight shooting the weapon is brought to the controlling eye. In getting the handgun to the controlling eye, the wrist must be bent, and after so many repetitions, the wrist becomes programmed to be crooked. If the same shooter points the weapon, lacking time or light to sight, they have a very high probability of shooting very low or somewhere in the area of the target. To correct this potential problem a simple exercise can be used.

Place the handgun down along the leg, *(See Fig. 48)* tighten the grip and then move the weapon to a mark on the target and the wrist will likely be straight. Continue this exercise until you can draw the handgun from a holster, point it at an object on the wall and it will be level to a target at chest level, a second person can confirm this relationship.

**Option #3—Programming the Fit**

*Fig. 48. Handgun Set Straight Down Along the Leg, Trigger Finger Straight, Wrist Straight*

*Fig. 49. Pointed Handgun With A Level Barrel*

As a training person I have watched thousands of shooters shoot millions of rounds of fire on steel targets. I always stand to the right side of the shooter or the left side of those left handed people. When we begin training, I assist each shooter in setting the handgun to the target so it will shoot where pointed. The accuracy I train for is to have the initial shot no more than two inches from a point of concentration at a distance of 15 feet. In shooting a handgun with a four-inch barrel, the accuracy I work towards is:

### Accuracy formula:

$$\frac{\text{(Length of the Barrel)} = (4)}{\text{(Error of the Barrel)} = (X)} \quad \frac{\text{(Distance to the target)} = (15'\times12'')}{\text{(Error of the Bullet)} = (2)}$$

Cross multiplying and solving for X

$$\frac{4}{X} = \frac{(180)}{2}$$

$180X = 8 \quad X = .044 =$ maximum error at the end of the barrel

## A Learning Experience

Proper fit and focus can be programmed in as few as 100 to 150 rounds of fire, which would be 20 to 30 repetitions at 5 shots per repetition.

In learning to accurately point the handgun, each shooter will go through three levels in learning:

1. The Hands on Level
2. Hands Off—Becoming independent of the instructor
3. Final level of aggression!

The initial level will be a beginners level totally dependent on the instructor to teach them fit, skill and mind-set.

The second learning level will normally begin after the shooter has fired 100 to 150 rounds. This level in learning will be that in which students begin to want to shoot without the instructors assistance. In beginning a level of independence, the cone of fire may double its diameter the first time a student shoots. The next round of five shots will normally have a smaller cone of fire, then as the shooter becomes more independent of the instructor, which will occur at about the third or fourth round of 5 shots, the student will become totally independent of their instructor and hopefully the cone of fire will return to the dimension it was when they were in the hands-on phase of the initial learning level.

After completing the second level in learning, students quickly move into the final level in learning and become aggressive in their moves and actions. This final level in learning should not come unless the gun fits and the shooter has control of their point of concentration during the time the gun is discharging.

## Range Activity

### The Pointing Position

In pointing the handgun, where a shooter holds the gun relative to the eyes can vary from a most natural pointing position at chest level to a position above or below the chest. I have found that if the handgun is held below a natural pointing position, like the hip, accuracy is lost. I've also found that if a shooter holds the handgun higher than chest level the shooter may or may not lose accuracy. It all depends on whether holding the weapon in the immediate area of the controlling eye has a magnetic effect on the focal point of the eye by drawing it off the pre-selected point of impact.

An isosceles triangle is one with two equal sides. It is my feeling that holding the arms straight away from the body is uncomfortable, and it can make a shot go low. I prefer to take the tension off the arms by pulling them in to a slight bowed position. With this arm position, you can hold the bullets as steady as you can hold the eye.

A True Isosceles Arm Position

*Fig. 50. Uncomfortable and apt to make the shots go low with the arms fully extended.*

# POINT-SHOOTING HANDGUNS + 129

**A Modified Isosceles Arm Position**

Fig. 51. Arms not fully extended—A Most Natural Way to hold the Handgun

**A Basic Body Position— Modified Isosceles Arm Position**

Fig. 52. John Solheim. A Beginning Stance, Handgun held in the Modified Isosceles Position

**Taller Than Normal Shooter**

*Fig. 53. Setting on a stool puts the taller shooter down to my level for programming the fit. Once the wrist is programmed to hold the handgun so it will shoot where the shooter is looking, the wrist position locks in for a target at any angle or height relative to the shooter.*

**Beginning to Learn—Shooting the First Box of Ammunition**

*Fig. 54. Programming the fit for William Shafer in the desert of Lordsburg, New Mexico*

*Fig. 55. William Shafer, March 17, 2003 Lordsburg, New Mexico*

## 150 Rounds of Fire Later—A New Member of the Club

After learning how to point the handgun, I do not advocate shooting consistently from one side or the other as a set standard. The habit of always shooting off the right or the left side becomes subconscious, then, shooting off a different side is apt to give you the feeling that you can't shoot because your not in that proper stance position. We best learn to shoot from any body position you could be in at the time the weapon is needed.

## A Beginning Handgun Shooting Sequence

Set up a target with a ½″ mark in the center of the chest, back off a distance of 15 feet, load the handgun with five rounds, focus the mark on the chest, bring the handgun to a modified Isosceles position and point it at the mark and fire one, two, three, four and five shots. When you finish, you should still be looking at the mark. **Do not chase the bullets, do not adjust the weapon, just remember:**

> The dimension of the cone of fire will be equal to the total deviation of your point of concentration.

Where the bullets go is fit, how the bullets go determines your level of skill. The more you shift your focal point, in chasing the bullets, the larger the cone of fire. Patch the holes in the paper target or take off all the marks on a steel target, except one to focus on for the next round of fire.

Repeat the above sequence until you've fired the first 50 rounds, always telling yourself what you're going to do before you bring the weapon to the final position and fire.

**Remember:** To learn, conscious thought must come before and after we shoot but it should not come during the period of time we're shooting.

Repeat the beginning handgun shooting sequence again using the second box of ammunition. Because of the learning curve, the second box of ammunition will be easier to shoot than the initial box.

### Take a 10 Minute Break

Lets begin firing the third box of ammunition. Somewhere in shooting this box, experienced pistol shooters normally move into the final learning level.* While shooting the third box of ammunition, I check the fit by

---

*Border Patrol Agents have all gone thru one of the Border Patrol Academy's. In the academy firearms training program each student agent will shoot 2000+ rounds of ammunition. These people are not new shooters, only new to point-shooting.

looking to see how the student sets the handgun to the mark on the target. For a mark the same height as the shooters arm, the gun barrel will appear to my eye as being level. If the pistol feels like it's on the mark to me and it already feels like it's on the mark to the shooter, I let the student fire the first, second, third, fourth and last shot and if the bullets are on the money, I'm happy.

Now the student is ready to move slowly into the final learning level and that is a level of aggression but I don't talk about it, when the student is ready it will happen. If the student is not ready, they must continue shooting the beginning handgun shooting sequence until they have control of the fit, and control over the dimension of the cone of fire. If the student is shooting low after 150–200 rounds of fire. *(Refer to page 123 Reprogramming the Subconscious)*

In the act of point shooting, shooters will receive a feedback before the bullets leave the gun as to whether or not the bullets will be in or out of control. It's subconscious feedback and it's based on a relationship between the focal point of the eye relative to the point of impact at the time the trigger is pulled.

## Exercise to Sharpen the Eye of the Shooter

All shooters in a class can steady their eye to a point of impact while someone else is shooting. We do it by focusing the same mark on the target used by the shooter. The focal point of the eye should be steady to the mark from the beginning to the end of firing. We only intend to program a period of time lasting from two to four seconds long. Work with this exercise until the focal point of your eye is steady to the mark from the start to the finish of shooting.

When at home I never practice handgun shooting but I know what I have to do to fire the bullets touching at a distance of 15 feet. I don't believe the fit of the gun changes once it's programmed into the subconscious, I believe it's the shooters focus that's apt to change after a long period of time without firing the gun. I do know I get out of shooting what I put into it, nothing more, nothing less.

## Walk and Draw Sequences

Walk and draw sequences will teach the shooter to shoot from any position the body could be in at the time the weapon is needed. From different angles relative to a paper or steel target a shooter sequence would be to walk, stop, identify the target, draw, and fire 5 rounds. I vary my shooting distance from 3 to 7 yards and incorporate the "Fighting Stance" which people instinctively revert to in times of stress.

## The Fighting Stance

Put a ruler to the plane of the barrel and see where the gun sets relative to the eyes of the shooter.

Fig. 56. Jim Gregg

# Learning to Shoot from Any Position the Body Could Be In At the Time Lethal Force is Necessary

"The Yakima Reverse"— The only position you can be in and shoot 360 degrees

*Fig. 57. Five shots touching at a shooting distance of 14 ft. Leslie Robb, U.S. Customs, San Angelo, TX. Shooting .45 Caliber S & W 1992*

136 + THE GREGG METHOD OF FIRE CONTROL

Fig. 58. Officer down, suspect straightaway

POINT-SHOOTING HANDGUNS + 137

Fig. 59. Sitting

Fig. 60. I just don't know the application of this "stance" with the exception of knowing that in using the "Gregg Method of Fire Control", you can shoot from any position.

## Multiple Targets

The speed of fire is controlled by the speed of focus. The time it takes to see the next target, focus where you want the shot to go and fire, it should all happen at once.

## Shooting on the Move

Shooting on the move and accuracy don't seem to go together. Accuracy is relative to distance to the target and the skill of the shooter. If a person would walk down a road and look at an object ahead, then point a finger at the object, then, as long as the shooters focus stays on the object, the finger or a handgun will also. We, however, get a lot of movement in a weapon when walking or running and any officer having accuracy under these conditions should be thankful to none other than the Lord above!

## Speed of Fire

With the eyes on the target, the speed of fire is controlled by the speed of focus and the speed of the draw. If we shoot before we focus the point of impact, shots tend not to be in control. If we do not shoot after we focus the point of impact, the conscious mind tends to activate, the eyes dilate and shots can go anywhere. Never reduce your focus to a point of impact unless you intend to shoot.

There are three steps in shooting and these are: See the target, focus the point of impact and fire the shot, it should all happen at once.

Speed of fire can be handicapped by the speed of the draw. Holsters are classed based on their ability to retain the handgun. Levels of retention range from a level one holster, which has the least security level to a level three holster which has the highest ability to retain the weapon. It is very important to be familiar with the holster you wear as familiarity in drawing the weapon will affect your speed of fire especially if you wear a level three holster and can't get your gun out when you really need it.

I have a friend, a deputy in our sheriff's department; who ordered a level three holster. When it arrived he put it on his duty belt, added his pistol, tried to get the gun out and it didn't come out.

When all else fails, read the instructions! He did and it was not easy to make a three step draw compared to his old class one holster, so he decided to do ten draws in the morning, before he went to work and ten draws in the evening before taking off his uniform. After a couple of weeks it became easier to make a three step draw and he felt it was becoming instinctive and his gun was more secure than it was in the older level one holster.

One night my friend was in his patrol car making his rounds when he got a call that an alarm had gone off at a local potato plant. Pat proceeded to the plant and pulled in front of the building. In getting out of the vehicle he noticed a backup vehicle coming. When the other deputy arrived it happened to be another deputy who also ordered a level three holster but never took the time to really work with it until he got used to it.

Both officers proceed to search the area and it wasn't long before they encountered a suspect who came at them with a three foot length of galvanized pipe. Instinctively, Pat drew his pistol, pointed it at the suspect and told him that if he took another step, he'd kill him, that got his attention. Pat then told his backup to keep the fellow covered while he put the cuffs on and he heard no response from the other deputy. Pat looked to see the deputy still trying to get his gun out of the level three holster.

It was later felt that if the backup deputy had responded first he might have been killed by the suspect, recently released from a mental institution. Speed of fire is based on the speed of focus and the speed of the draw.

## Pursuit and Shoot Sequences

Point shooters should shoot as good after a pursuit as they would if a pursuit had not been made. This phenomenon is not conditioned, it just happens to all shooters. Running may bother the cone of fire the first time a pursuit is made but do the run a time or two again and the cone of fire should reduce to its normal dimension.

During the time the weapon is discharging, shooters should have no sensation of having made a pursuit as the system instinctively stops breathing during the time shots are fired. If, however, the shooter is way out of condition and isn't up to running 50 to 100 yards without possible having a stroke, then I don't believe the system will stop breathing during the critical period of time the gun is firing, this particular shooter will end up with diarrhea of the bullets.

## An Awesome Feat

On December 13, 1999 Agents Russell Long (Left) and Noel Cantu, USBP Laredo, TX shot two triangular 5 shot groups after running 80 yards on a two man Pursuit and Shoot sequence.

Fig. 61. *"Don't mess with Texans"*

## Accuracy in Point-Shooting

Fig. 62. *On the 6th day of April 2000, Jason Violette, U.S.B.P., Comstock, Texas became the 1000th member of the "Hole in One Club"*

POINT-SHOOTING HANDGUNS + 141

Fig. 63. Daryl Anderson, Yukon Renewable Resources, Watson Lake, Yukon Territories. Shot five bullets touching, 15 feet from the target, July 5, 1994

Fig. 64. Diana Ortiz, U.S.B.P., Carrizo Springs, TX fired two one inch groups with her .40 Caliber Beretta from a distance of 15 feet. December 1, 2000

142 + THE GREGG METHOD OF FIRE CONTROL

Fig. 65. Tom Wacker, Blaine Sector Chief, U.S. Border Patrol Fired 5 bullets touching at a distance of 15 feet, 1994

## Tightest .45 Caliber Group

Fig. 66. Jack Bourgeois, Lafayette Parish Sheriff's Department shot five bullets touching 15 feet from the target with his .45 caliber pistol, point shooting. The dimension of the cone of fire was measured at one inch. 1991

POINT-SHOOTING HANDGUNS + 143

*Fig. 67. Cathy Edwards, U.S.B.P. Laredo, TX shot 5 bullets touching at a distance of 15 feet. September 18, 2000*

*Fig. 68. Katherine Thibeault, U.S.B.P. Del Rio, TX shot five bullets touching at a distance of 15 feet, March 16, 2000*

*Fig. 69. Carmen Mirabile, U.S.B.P., Del Rio, TX shot 5 bullets touching, 15 feet from the target. March 16, 2000*

*Fig. 70. Rosanne Smith, U.S.B.P., Del Rio, TX shot five bullets touching 15 feet from the target. January 13, 1998*

POINT-SHOOTING HANDGUNS + 145

Fig. 71. Wayne Ternes, Montana State Prison, shot five bullets touching at a distance of 15 ft.

Fig. 72. Accepting a challenge, Jim Gregg, Moses Lake, WA shot 5 bullets touching at a distance of 15 feet with a borrowed .40 Caliber Glock pistol, Burlington Northern School, Springfield, Missouri, 1993

146 + THE GREGG METHOD OF FIRE CONTROL

Fig. 73. Joe Tammen, PAIC, Lordsburg Station, New Mexico, March 17, 2003

Fig. 74. Chuck Akeroyd, U.S.B.P. Pilot, Del Rio, Texas Five shots touching, March 28, 2000

POINT-SHOOTING HANDGUNS + 147

Fig. 75. Michael Turk, U.S.B.P., Eagle Pass, Texas, Fired a perfect Hole in One while laying on his back, February 15, 1992

Fig. 76. Howard Anster, U.S.B.P., San Angelo, Texas, five shots from 15 feet with a .40 Caliber Beretta, 1993

148 + THE GREGG METHOD OF FIRE CONTROL

Fig. 77. My nephew, Tim Gregg had never shot a pistol before this first day of handgun training. He made the Hole in One club shooting the third box ammunition. March 31, 1996

Fig. 78. Edward George (Right Front), U.S. Customs, Air Branch, San Angelo, Texas, five shots touching at a distance of 15 feet, January 16, 1993

After learning how to point a handgun or shotgun, every move you make should be instinctive and done without conscious thought. You shouldn't have to think to draw the pistol, you shouldn't have to think to point it, you shouldn't have to think about how to see the target and you don't have to think to pull the trigger. Whether you pull the trigger or not will be based on what you see as a deadly threat to yourself or another innocent person.

## Effective Distances in Point-Shooting

I always begin training at a distance of 15 feet from a target simply because that's where the action takes place. All training with the handgun is within 21 feet of the target. I would say the average working range for the average student point shooting would be 30 feet. We have had miss and out games that have been won at a distance of 52 yards.

**STATISTICS TELL US THAT:**
- 95% of the time the adversary will be within 21 feet of the officer
- 70% of the time the adversary will be between 5 to 10 feet of the officer
- Two thirds of the time it will happen during the nighttime.

The effective distance relative to accuracy in point shooting is limited by the shooters level of concentration. With perfect mindset, I have shot 5″ groups with my Glock Model 22, .40 Caliber, from the 25 yard line.

The best point shooting I have ever done was at a demonstration I gave in 1973 out of Ellensburg, Washington in front of about 50 police and deputy sheriffs. Before that day my shooting was always done within 20 feet of the target so all the shooting I did during the demonstration was done within 20 feet of the target.

At the end of the demonstration, one of the officers asked me how far back I could go and still shoot accurately. I answered the question by saying that you can shoot a lot further back and I turned around began to walk back and forgot to stop. When I did the focal length of the 32″

high steel target was about 2 inches. I took a second looked at the target and got to thinking that the only thing that has changed from shooting at the 5 yard line was the focal length of the target, so if I see the target the same way I see it at the 5 yard line why should anything change? I loaded 5 rounds in my Model 28 Smith and Wesson, brought it up to my firing position, visualized to where I wanted the shots to go and began talking to the target by saying that I want all the shots to go perfect to the center of the plate as I fired one, two, three, I felt the fourth shot slip, corrected by mind to zero and the last shot hit right by the initial three bullets fired. The cops let out a YAHOO! One got a camera, another got a 100 foot tape and measured the distance at 54 feet, I was impressed. On the way home I got to thinking about how accurately I held the revolver to shoot a group that was only 2″ wide and 3″ high with just a single shot out of the group by about 4".

I solved the question by thinking it was a proportion.

$$\frac{\text{(Length of the Barrel)} = (6")}{\text{(Error of the Barrel)} = (X)} \qquad \frac{\text{(Distance to the target)} = (54 \times 12)}{\text{(Error of the Bullet)} = (2")}$$

I cross multiplied and solved for X and the total error at the end of the barrel was .0185 inches. Standard deviation would be .009 inches.

I then knew I could hold the bullets as steady as I could hold my conscious mind—*mindset*. By talking to the target, I preoccupied the subconscious to prevent a function of the conscious.

## Shooting at Night

Shooting at night is different than daytime shooting because of the lack of light.

The first color we see at night is white. We can see white on black and black on white but we cannot see black on black or white on white.

The eye doesn't see, it's the brain that sees, the eye has to produce an image in order for the brain to see. The eye won't focus unless it has something to focus on, so how are we going to accurately point and shoot a weapon at night if our concentration becomes dilated?

The key to shooting as good or even better at night than daytime lies in the word game. Focus and concentration are synonymous so if the eye won't focus we can set a point of concentration by visualization, this will set the point of impact for the first shot, then as long as the mind stays steady (mindset), the rest of the shots will impact the immediate area of the first shot. At this point in shooting, shooters will feel their shots as steady or unsteady as they fire and when the flashlight is turned on to read the bullets, shots will print the function or non-function of the conscious mind.

## Potential Nighttime Accuracy

Years ago, I had a school in Bremerton, Washington. In one of the classes I had a student shoot the tightest group I have ever seen with a .38 caliber handgun firing wadcutters. This fellow shot a group of five shots onto a steel target at a distance of 13 feet that I could cover with a quarter. I often wondered if he had been into the study of Zen!

Night Shooting a Ported Glock Pistol

*Fig. 79. Willie Castleberry (Ret), U.S.B.P. San Angelo, TX, shooting his personally owned pistol. 1992*

152 + **THE GREGG METHOD OF FIRE CONTROL**

*Fig. 80. Shooting is always done in the darkness of night, then I turn a light on to read the bullets.*

POINT-SHOOTING HANDGUNS + 153

Night Shooting

"Hole in One"

Fig. 81. Five shots touching fifteen feet from the target. James W. Doyle, U.S.B.P., Del Rio, TX, December 23, 1997

Fig. 82. Five shots touching fifteen feet from the target at night time. Troy Meredith, U.S.B.P, Carrizo Springs, TX, May 24, 1997

## A Nighttime Sequence

In a nighttime sequence we walk, stop, identify a target, draw, visualize a point on the target, set the handgun to your point of concentration and fire the bullets without wondering where they are going, mindset. You must believe your shots are going right where you want them to go. If the shooter questions where the bullets are going, shots generally go down in a curve from the initial point of impact.

Nighttime shooting is as good or better than daytime shooting because of what a shooter doesn't see. In daylight, it's what the shooter sees that makes them do what they do and if they didn't see it they wouldn't do it and that's chasing the bullets with the line of sight as they impact the target.

At night, the distance to the target is dramatically shortened by the lack of light. I try not to use artificial light to produce an image of the target unless I have a black on black condition, which I find in a forest or brushy area. If I can get an image of a target to shoot at, we shoot. The image can be the whole target, the top half, the bottom half or lastly I can get an image by turning on the parking lights of a patrol car and moving it back or forward until we barely see something to shoot at.

At night, shooters go through the same sequences that are done during the hours of daylight, except pursuits. Shooters have a handicap at night that they don't have to contend during the daylight and that's the effect of the first shot on vision. The first shot flame cycle takes all vision to the target away so the only time we can see is before and after shots are fired.

## Mindset

Most shooters have heard of mindset. You have to have mindset to listen, you have to have mindset for the eyes to focus, and most importantly, in shooting, you have to have mindset during the time the weapon is firing, which may be one, two or three seconds of time. It all depends on how many shots are fired. Mindset is merely the act of clearing the conscious mind during the critical period of time the weapon is firing.

> You have to win the fight before the gun leaves the holster, you win it with confidence

## Shooters Games

The second day of training I like to have the class shoot a "Miss and Out". Shooting begins with a single shooter firing one shot from the 10 yard line, miss the target and you're out of the game. All shooting must be done without using sights, the pistol must be held at below eye level.

In the beginning the target will have nothing for the shooter to focus on so they have to visualize a spot in the center of the target. One at a time each shooter steps up and fires a single shot until all are finished. I pace off 10 feet further back from the target and add a marker to the ground and the first shooter again steps up, draws and fires one shot. After all shooters who hit the target finish, another 10 feet is added and shooters continue to hit the target or miss it until a single shooter is left.

The first time the game is played shooters drop out faster than the second time the game is played and the more they play a "miss and out" the better the shooters get and the greater distance they learn to shoot from. I had a class in Eagle Pass years ago and two Border Patrol rookies, two months out of the academy, backed up a distance of 52 yards before we had a winner!

## Snakes

At a going away party for Gordon Schneider, retiring Patrol Agent in Charge of the Eagle Pass, Texas Border Patrol Station, one of the fellows came up to me and was smiling from ear to ear and said "Jim, I was in your class a year ago and you told us that if we wanted to kill a rattlesnake you have to focus the bottom of the head as you draw and fire. Months later I was out on patrol in heavy mesquite and prickly pear cactus and I heard the rattle. I looked and there he was four feet away, I drew my gun, pointed it at the head, focused the bottom of the head and BLAM, the head on that critter just exploded, I still can't believe it, that .40 caliber sure does a job on them snakes".

## Ants

On the second day of a two-day shooting school at the Eagle Pass Range, the class was shooting great and I wanted them to enjoy some killing. I previously noticed an anthill close to the 15 yard concrete line. I borrowed a Beretta .40 Caliber and wanted to show the class how to kill an ant. I loaded the chamber, set the gun to the ant, focused the bottom of an ant running along the concrete about 12 feet away and BLAM, the ant disappeared. I focused the bottom of another ant and BLAM, it went to "slab city". I shot five ants in a row. Then I lined up the class the same distance away from the concrete and after a couple of shots they got the picture and we had a lot of fun killing ants. I figured if they could kill an ant at 12 feet they wouldn't have any trouble hitting their target in the heat of battle.

## The Instructors Memories

The following pictures were taken out of Sierra Blanca, TX. Chris Bipley, U.S.B.P. shot five "Hole in One's" during two days of training, and followed up with a 20 shot group that measured just 2½ inches in diameter.

Fig. 83. Bipley #1

158 + THE GREGG METHOD OF FIRE CONTROL

Fig. 84. Bipley #2

Fig. 85. Bipley #3

POINT-SHOOTING HANDGUNS + 159

Fig. 86. Bipley #4

Fig. 87. Bipley #5

*Fig. 88. Bipley #6—Chris Bipley shot four, five shot groups around the same point of concentration. Sierra Blanca, TX, March 11, 1991.*

# BORDER PATROL MEMORIES

It is very important to understand what conditions a typical deadly encounter takes place for the law enforcement officer. I am enclosing a report of narcotics apprehended over an 11 month period in the year 2000 by U.S. Border Patrol agents working out of the Eagle Pass, Texas Station. I am also enclosing several reports of some deadly shooting confrontations and drug busts that have occurred on the southern border of the United States in the past.

The more you understand about the use of firearms the better you are in understanding their purpose. You can sight, aim or point any weapon and whether you would use any one method over another would depend on conditions that exist at the time the weapon is needed. No one method of shooting a handgun applies in all conditions of use. Every lawman yearns for a method of controlling their weapon 24/7.

—Jim Gregg

*What the Border Patrol taught me about firearms and shootings was that how well you knew your equipment and how to use it was more important than what type of equipment you had.*

*I can remember Kent Williams (Retired Firearms Instructor) demonstrating that through practice he could load six from his belt loop (without looking) as fast as a classmate of mine could load the same gun with a speed loader. His message was that practice with what you carried was more critical than what it was you carried. I warned my young agents that they had to make up for the advantage that their opposition almost certainly would have in a shooting on the border and that was that they (the bad guy) knew in advance there was going to be a shooting. Whatever prepared them (my agents) to quickly deliver one well placed round from the holster, without warning, was useful to them.*

*Qualification scores did not necessarily equate with performance in real shooting situations. Your training, Jim, was the big part of my perception of this facet of the Border Patrol job.*

—Gordon Schneider, Retired<br>
Patrol Agent in Charge<br>
U.S. Border Patrol Station<br>
Eagle Pass, TX

## EAGLE PASS STATION—DRUG SEIZURES 2000
### (Jan thru Nov)

| MONTH | MARIJUANA LBS. | COCAINE | HEROIN | NO. OF SEIZURES |
|---|---|---|---|---|
| JAN | 3403 | | | 10 |
| FEB | 2137.4 | | | 10 |
| MAR | 6774.4 | | | 7 |
| APR | 1209 | | | 6 |
| MAY | 901.4 | | | 7 |
| JUN | 1647.7 | | | 5 |
| JUL | 1042.6 | | | 8 |
| AUG | 1238.1 | | | 7 |
| SEP | 194.4 | 360 | | 3 |
| OCT | 1790.9 | | | 7 |
| NOV | 2295.6 | | 12.8oz. | 13 |
| TOTALS | 22,634.5 lbs Marijuana | 360lbs Cocaine | 12.8oz. Heroin | 83 Seizures |

Note: Averaging the above figures roughly show agents caught about 2057 pounds a month or about 68 pounds a day. The Eagle Pass Station's 225 Agents *(mas o menos)* made 81,000 arrests in fiscal year 2000 along the same 56 miles of river. The Eagle Pass Station was the most productive station in Texas for arrests during that time.

## Maurice Dixon and Warren O'Neal Incident

*July 4, 1946*
As told by Jerrell Edmison

Maurice Dixon and B.Warren O'Neal were working downriver from Fabens near Tornillo on the John Segulia farm. They had decided to lay-in near a flume that carried canal water across a drainage ditch about 300 yards from the Rio Grande River. It was called the Vince Segulia crossing, and smugglers had used it for years, as it was widely known that in crossing the flume, one could transverse both barriers simultaneously, and proceed directly inland.

Both officers spotted two men crossing the river shortly after dusk, and they could see that both were heavily laden with bundles. They hid in some cattails, and after the men had crossed the flume and reached a rise on the other side, Maurice stepped out and shined his flashlight on both smugglers. He identified himself, and told them in Spanish to lay down the bundles and put their hands up. Warren stood beside Maurice, and it appeared that the smugglers were going to comply. The lead Mexican was a large man, about six feet tall, and as he slowly started down with his load, both officers heard a ratchety sound, a muffled but fast click, click, click. Maurice went for his revolver while instinctively turning his body sideways, his left shoulder towards the sound.

The calm evening air exploded with the sound of a pistol shot, and Maurice made a sharp grunting sound as a bullet pierced his abdomen. He returned the fire with four fast shots with his .38, and as the smuggler fell back into the bundles of contraband, he fired two more shots. Warren had also drawn his weapon, and the other alien grabbed the barrel, forcing it downward in an attempt to wrestle it away. As the two tumbled down the incline toward the flume, Warren fired his pistol six times in fast succession, emptying his revolver into the lower torso of his combatant.

"Madre Mia," he screamed as he scrambled back up toward his fallen comrade and his own weapon, which he had accidentally dropped. Warren grabbed at his feet but he shook free, and as he topped the berm, a wounded Maurice was waiting for him with the dead smuggler's own weapon, the hammer cocked back and ready to fire. Maurice had no way of knowing who had prevailed in the scuffle below him. He only knew that the man coming at him was not his partner. The coup de grace was swift and sure, with the .44 caliber bullet entering the smuggler's head below the right temple.

A total of eighteen shots were fired and it was all over in about forty-five seconds. B. Warren radioed Sector as he drove Maurice to the hospital, and the dispatcher relayed the news to Assistant Chief, John Swanson. Mr. Swanson telephoned our house and talked to Dad, and the strangest sensation I had yet experienced occurred when I heard Dad tell Mother Maurice was wounded. I think it was the first time that my young psyche wholly separated childhood fantasy from reality, and I remember trembling as Dad left for the scene of the shooting.

The newspaper described the incident as "...a desperate Rio Grande gun battle reminiscent of prohibition days....the smugglers were carrying 40 bottles of assorted liquors, 50 lbs. of sugar, 83 packages of cigarettes, and a large bundle of marijuana. It was apparent that neither of them had any intention of surrendering to anyone that night as evidenced by the pistol hidden and held in the ready position beneath the sack of contraband liquor.

Maurice's injury, thank God, was not life threatening. His instinctive reaction to the cocking of the old .44 single action pistol probably saved his life. The bullet pierced the stomach area, but only grazed the abdominal wall. Both he and B.Warren received commendations from Attorney General Clark and Commissioner of Immigration, Carusi. Warren was commended specifically for his courage in struggling with the smuggler while preventing him from seizing his revolver.

As to the old pistol, I've got it. It's the very one fired by Maurices's adversary that fateful night, and by Maurice to finish off the other smuggler. Several people had possession of it during the early years prior to Dad, and ultimately me, acquiring it. As I sit here looking at it, cocking back the hammer and reminiscing about the past, I am struck with the sentiment that, aside from photographs, there are probably too few mementos exemplifying the remarkable accomplishments of the Patrol Inspectors of that era. This old relic qualified as an heirloom of sorts, and instead of being stuck in the back of a locker, it should be brought out into the open to somehow serve as a reminder of the daily risks faced by officers of the U.S. Border Patrol in general, as well as the peril encountered by those two brave Patrolmen in particular.

July 4, 1996 will mark the 50$^{th}$ anniversary of the incident, and I think that would be a fitting date for me to turn over the pistol to the Border Patrol Museum in El Paso where it can join all the other artifacts representative of our agencies' esteemed past. My son will soon be joining the ranks of the Border Patrol, and I can only hope that as the torch is passed on, he can come to appreciate my generation's achievement as much as I venerate my father's era, as the U.S. Border Patrol continues its mission of protecting the boundaries of this great nation.

—Jerrell Edmison

## Azrack-Newton Abduction-BPA Murders

*As told by Gordon Schneider, Retired Border Patrol Officer*

I first came in the Border Patrol in 1978 and there were still residual warnings to agents resulting from the Azrack-Newton murder in 1967. There were two young agents working Oak Grove checkpoint out of Temecula Station. One had about a year in and the other was just out of the academy, I think. They were told to check every vehicle on a rural road in the mountains West of Borrego Springs.

A military ambulance (Power Wagon?) with some guys in military uniforms came through the point. They waved them thru. After discussion they decided to run it down and check it. When they did, they were taken into custody by suspects with automatic weapons. The truck was a ruse and the suspects had a multi-hundred pound load of marijuana.

The suspects took the agents to a remote cabin near Anza, handcuffed them to a stove and executed them with their own guns. Today there is an award for heroism in the patrol called the Azrack-Newton Award. When I went through the Academy, eleven or twelve years after the event, we were admonished strongly to never give up our weapons under any circumstances, even if your partner was captured, or we would die by them. Azrack-Newton was pointed at as proof of this.

In El Centro Sector we were trained that if the officer on primary (checking cars) ever dropped to the pavement it was a signal to shoot everybody in the car. We were also told (and I always did) to talk to all partners at the start of a shift together to let them know that you would not give up your gun even if they were being held at gunpoint to get you to. You would agree that at the critical moment you were going to fire and they should do whatever they could to help (drop or fight back or whatever) Azrack-Newton was a biggie in my training experience.

Readers Digest did a multi-part article on it in 1967, I think. Told the whole story in detail. After the guys did not come in after the shift there was a three or four day manhunt for them involving FBI and numerous agencies. Ab Taylor and Dana Ellsworth were among Chula Sectors (then named) ace trackers. Ab ran the unit and Dana was one of his fair-haired boys. On the third of fourth day of the search, they found the bodies in the remote cabin. The FBI cordoned it off. Ab and Dana (and perhaps other trackers) were brought in to, one by one, cut a circle around the cabin for sign in and out.

They both told me it was quite eerie to make those cuts under those circumstances. The bodies were still as they had fallen. They did not know if the suspects were still there hiding among the huge rock outcroppings that surrounded the cabin. Both Dana and Ab commented that there were a lot of grown men crying on that scene and that it was hard to look at the bodies in the Border Patrol uniforms. One had a single shot to the head (the first to die) the other had several wounds, as he knew what was coming and struggled.

Ab, as the tracking unit boss, worked closely with the FBI boss on that deal and had high praise for the man. Ab said the man's nickname was "Rack-Rack", as he liked a shotgun in arrest situations. Ab was convinced that "Rack-Rack" took him along later in the case when they got a lead on where the marijuana and suspects might be just so Ab could be present when "Rack-Rack" loosed the shotgun on them. It turned out the suspects weren't there though.

—Gordon Schneider, Retired

## Alan W. Gordon Shooting Incident

*0300 Hours 08-09-68, Canyon City, California*

On August 8, 1968 about 6 PM I talked to S.P.I. Fleming at the Chula Vista office. He told me that a load of aliens were to cross the border about six miles east of Tecate and be picked up in the Canyon City, California area between 4 and 6 AM on 08-09-68. I passed the information on to S.P.I. Wells of the Campo station and he agreed I should take up a still-watch position along the railroad tracks and try to apprehend the guide as he returned to Mexico and also let the other units know when the load was in the area. We knew from past information and sign-cutting activities what route the aliens would take.

I got into position about 11 PM on 08-08-68 about 100 yards South of Highway 94 and in the brush about 10 yards east of the tracks. About 3:00 AM on 08-09-68 I observed a single person with a pack on his back and carrying a bundle in his left hand walking past my position going north along the railroad tracks. I watched this person walk almost to the railroad bridge at the highway and heard a sound like something being tossed into the brush. This person then returned to a dirt trail just north of me, turned and walked to the highway.

I did not want to give my position away at that time so I called inspector D. Lindemann and told him what I had seen. He came to the area but was unable to locate the suspect. I left my position and assisted him with the search and then helped him start his vehicle after the battery had gone dead. After we started his vehicle and he had returned toward Canyon City, I observed a white Camaro pass through the area. From the actions of the car I felt that the driver was looking for someone or something. I went back to my position and again called Inspector Lindemann. He had observed the vehicle and was in the process of following it toward Campo. He later returned and said the vehicle was clean but would bear watching.

About 4:15 AM I heard someone walking and observed another person walking north along the track past my position. This person was also carrying a pack on his back. The subject turned toward the highway on the dirt trail just north of my position. I felt that by this time, due to all the previous activity in the area, the aliens were not going to show, so I left my position and ran toward the subject. When I was within about 25 yards of the subject I called for him to stop. He stopped and set the pack on the ground and turned toward me crying "Don't take me in, don't arrest me I have a family." Subject looked very glassy eyed, as if he was under the influence of drugs and was very nervous. I told him to turn around and sit down and that he was under arrest. The subject turned and started to sit, then jumped up and took a step or two toward me again pleading not to take him in.

About this time I saw a snub nose revolver lying on the ground near the pack. I drew my service revolver and told the subject to stop or I would shoot. The subject stopped and I laid my flashlight and nightstick on the ground, picked up the revolver and put it in my pocket. I again told the person to turn around and sit down. He turned around and put his left hand behind his back as if to let me put the cuffs on him. I opened the cuffs with my left hand put one on his left wrist and was reaching for his right wrist with my left hand still holding the cuffs with my fingers. As I touched his right arm he spun around and grabbed my hand and my revolver. We fell to the ground, myself on the bottom. I somehow got my foot or leg between us and pushed the subject away, I'm not sure how far. The subject then was on top of me again still with his hand on my gun. I fired two shots.

The subject fell to the ground crying "Oh my God you shot me, I'm going to die". He lay there groaning and I padded his pockets and found a small automatic pistol in his right front pocket. I removed it, putting it in my jacket pocket, and at the same time pulled a small revolver holster from his waist- band and tossed it on the ground. I picked up the snub nose again and put it in my pocket. I saw that the subject was still alive so I rolled him over to see how bad he was hit. I saw the wound in his left side, in the chest area. I ran back to my still watch position and tried to call Inspector Lindemann by walkie-talkie. I ran back to the subject still trying to contact Inspector Lindemann. I decided the battery was dead so I fired another shot into the air hoping Inspector Lindemann would hear it.

I waited about a minute and then ran to the highway on the west to Canyon City where I used a phone and called the office in Chula Vista. I told S.P.I. Jones what had happened and to send an ambulance and to notify the C.P.I. and S.P.I. Wells. I then returned to the scene and waited until the other officer arrived.

—Alan W. Gordon, I.P.I.

## East Desert Shoot-Out

*By Bill Glenn with the indispensable help of the Agents involved*

*Ten little smugglers smuggling pot,*
*Some made it back and some did not.*

Funny how little things can cause big things, mused Jesse Shaw recently when we were reminiscing about our days in El Centro back in the 70's. On the evening shift of May 29, 1972, he and fellow Border Patrol Agents, Harold Slocumb and Bill Brunell were assigned to patrol the desert in separate jeeps. That night they were to work both the East and West deserts. That was a pretty big order for one shift. Duty Senior Carl Phillips had told them to take care of the East desert first. Bill and Harold set off to cut and rake out the drops along the All American Canal while Jesse drove on out to cut the drag road East to the sand dunes. Jesse had his unauthorized .30 caliber M-1 carbine with a thirty-round clip in his jeep, so when he crossed the canal at remote Drop #2, he paused briefly to do some target practice at the resident carp population.

About halfway through the shift the three finished East and rather than heading West right away they decided to regroup for a quick break behind a canal bank near the nearly deserted I-8 freeway. That pause gave fate the next hand to deal. While they were sipping lukewarm thermos coffee and listening to one of Harold's wild stories, they observed two cars approach from the East and attempt to make a U-turn across the sandy median. One got stuck, but the other made it across and parked on a frontage road, a well-known pickup spot. The three PA's pounced on both cars and neither driver could give a convincing reason for being there. That naturally set off some bells and whistles. Jesse had Harold and Bill secure the two drivers while he drove South to make another quick cut on the East end of the drag road. The desert there is mostly soft sand dotted with greasewood bushes.

Shortly, Jesse radioed the others that he had cut sign of eight or ten and was on the trail. As he followed the tracks, they began to change directions, the group apparently having spotted the light of the pursuing vehicle. Harold radioed that he was heading over to give Jesse a hand, but about then Jesse spotted something off to his right. Turning in that direction, his headlights played across six large white bags under a bush.

Beyond the bags he saw a row of men about thirty feet away aiming guns at him. He grabbed the mike and shouted, "Marijuana. They're armed," as the first volley hit. Jesse said it sounded like rocks pounding into the vehicle. He jammed his jeep in reverse and grabbing his carbine, bailed out the door, rolling into the desert sand. As he did so, he saw a shadowy figure skirting around to his right in an attempt to flank the empty jeep. The man was in a low, almost duck-walk position and apparently hadn't seen Jesse abandon the vehicle. Jesse took a quick shot with his carbine and saw the man go down.

The abandoned jeep continued in reverse in a slow arc that played the headlights over Jesse as he was seeking cover. The tendency at night is to shoot low and fortunately the smugglers were doing just that. Jesse said they were hitting so close to him that the bullets were knocking sand in his face. He said he felt a wave of anger and figured he was dead, but would take a few of them along for the ride. As he rolled away back into the darkness, the jeep's headlights suddenly went out. The vehicle had become the second victim of the battle.

*Fig. 89. 215 pounds marijuana (six bags) 10 mules, Grey's Wells, Jesse Shaw, Harold Slocum, Bill Brunell 05-29-72. (Print of original painting courtesty U.S. Border Patrol, El Centro Sector Training)*

Jesse then began to return fire, aiming just to the right of the muzzle flashes of the smugglers' guns. (He was hoping they were right handed, he said.) It was fortunate that he had his carbine. As Jesse put it later, "Everyone knows we only have six shots before we have to stop and reload, so after I have fired more than six, the smugglers were ready to break it off and leave." Jesse had turned the tables. Now he was the aggressor.

All during the battle Jesse had been moving and firing in near total darkness except for muzzle flashes. When he had expended the fourteen rounds left over in his clip from his earlier "carp shoot", he drew his S&W .357 service revolver only to discover that it was packed with sand. He first tried to fire it double action, but it was jammed. Then he tried cocking it, but could not get the hammer back. He tried to open the cylinder, but it wouldn't budge. In frustration, he pushed the cylinder release once more and hit the cylinder hard against his knee and it finally opened. He spun the cylinder and blew on it to remove the sand, closed it and tried double action. No go, but he was able to cock the hammer. The concussion of his first shot freed up the mechanism and he was back in business. By the time he emptied his six pistol rounds, he was about a hundred yards from where the fight had begun. He had only six refills left and decided to head back to his jeep.

Early into the fight, his jeep had sustained a fatal wound to the engine block. The smuggler Jesse downed with his first shot had received a crippling leg wound and, unable to join his comrades, tried to commandeer the abandoned vehicle. As he was attempting to start it, Harold Slocumb arrived in the vicinity unaware that a gun battle had taken place. (He later explained that he had not been able to understand Jesse's radio warning but had sensed the urgency. Also, the noise of gunfire in the open desert does not carry well over engine noise.) Harold spotted Jesse's jeep and pulled up behind and to the right of it. In his headlights he could see that the occupant was wearing a blue bandanna on his head, so he knew it was not Jesse. The smuggler further confirmed that fact by exiting the jeep and pointing a semi-automatic pistol at Harold across the few feet separating them. Harold remembers him saying in Spanish to throw out his pistol, "*tira la pistola*". Thinking Jesse had been killed or wounded, Harold's response was immediate. Following the alternate meaning of *tirar* (to shoot), he drew his revolver and emptied it through his open window. Harold said the man was not a good target because he was partially shielded by the jeep's cab and he kept bobbing up and down like a jack-in-the-box. The smuggler managed to get off a shot or two before three of Harold's found their marks. The first hit the smuggler in his gun hand, the second in the neck and the third ricocheted off the jeep's rear bed and keyholed through the center of the smugglers forehead. He died instantly.

Bill Brunell, who had driven up from another direction and was ready to join in with his shotgun, observed the gun battle between Harold and the smuggler. He saw the smuggler drop heavily alongside the disabled jeep out of Harold's sight and said there was no doubt the man was dead by the way he fell. He shouted that information to Harold who was still looking for a target, having replaced his emptied revolver with a shotgun. He returned to his radio and called SPA Phillips, "Carl, you better come out here, I just had to kill a man".

Bill and Harold then turned their attention to finding Jesse, but it was Jesse who found them. When he got within shouting distance of the jeeps, he yelled out. "Hey, Harold bring me some ## ammo. (## is a code we used for emphasis) Said Harold later, "Those words were like music to our ears. We thought he had been killed". By this time the smugglers were well on their way back into Mexico, so they made no further attempt to pursue them.

The dead smugger had fallen so heavily against the side of Jesse's jeep that he came to rest partially under it. As the three turned their attention to the lifeless body, they saw that a sidewinder had crawled onto his chest, a rather strange sight to behold. It was later determined that Jesse's earlier shot had penetrated the man's right knee dead center from right to left, destroying the joint. That would account for his bobbing action when Harold was trying to zero in on him. Jesse figured the man had been trying to circle the jeep to catch him while he was still in the cab to finish him off at close range, but got "kneecapped" instead. It was not his night.

Jim Martin was working Anti-Smuggling near Gordon's Well, a couple of miles away, when the battle began, so was the first of many who responded. He said Jesse's radio call had been punctuated by the sounds of gunfire. Shortly after the battle ended, the desert began to get crowded with PA's from El Centro, Calexico and Yuma eager to pursue the smugglers South.

Their enthusiasm was reined in by Jim's better judgment when he pointed out that an armed invasion of Mexico was probably not a good idea.

The next morning tracks and other evidence revealed that there had been ten smugglers in all. They had been armed with semi-automatic weapons including .30 Carbine, 38 Super, .357, and 9 mm. Over fifty empty cases were recovered in the area. Jesse's jeep had been hit some fifteen times, many of the shots penetrating the cab after it had been vacated. The man killed at Jesse's jeep had been armed with a nickel-plated Colt .38 Super with an extended clip that could hold about twenty rounds. He had two or three left. Jesse noted that those calibers are restricted in Mexico to all but military and law enforcement. For that reason he is inclined to think there were policemen or other officials in the group.

In addition to the one Mexican smuggler killed at the scene, information was later received from the county coroner that two men had been admitted to the hospital in San Luis, Rio Colorado, with gunshot wounds and had died there. Two more had been found dead in the farming area in Ejido Zacatecasm directly South of where the battle took place. There were also unsubstantiated reports that some of the remaining had been wounded. Mexican *Judicales* captured two suspects in the desert early the next morning, then released them for "lack of evidence"—but only after relieving them of their firearms.

The day following the shooting, the Yuma Sun published a story identifying Harold by name and after that, he began receiving threatening telephone calls. He moved his family to San Diego and lived alone until the Service finally transferred him to San Clemente station. Word got out later that one of the victims was related to a big-time smuggler in Sonora who offered a $10,000 reward each for the deaths of the three Border Patrolmen. Fortunately, no one ever tried to collect.

On reflecting on the gun battle, Jesse was peeved at himself for leaving only fourteen rounds in a carbine clip that could hold thirty and not having brought spares with him that evening. He vowed never again to waste ammo on shooting carp. Last time I was out that way, the carp seemed happy about that.

—Bill Glenn

## Jewel Valley Shootout

*October 2, 1973, Alan W. Gordon S.P.A., Campo, California*

On October 1, 1973, about 8:00 PM I was called at my home by Agent R. Dunlap and informed that we had sensor traffic in Jewell Valley, South of Boulevard, California. I joined Agents Dunlap, R. Henderson and W. Miller in Boulevard about 9:00 PM. At 10:00 PM Agents Dunlap and Miller cut the sign of a group of aliens North bound through Jewell Valley. At this time Agent Dunlap reported he could count at least nine sets of tracks.

From the prior sign-cutting activities we felt we knew about where the group would go. Agents Dunlap and Henderson took-up a still-watch position on Interstate 8 where two prior groups using the same trail had crossed en route to the pick-up point. The pick-up point we had anticipated was a grove of oak trees on a jeep trail East of Live Oaks Springs Road and about ½ mile North of I-8 on the Manzanita Indian Reservation. Agents Gilbert, Bickley and Miller maintained a position on Ribbonwood Road and I-8, where they could observe traffic going into the area just East of Dunlap and Henderson and also assist them if necessary. They were later joined by Agent K. Summers about 12:00 midnight. I had taken-up a position on Live Oaks Springs Road where I could observe any traffic going into the pick-up area. I was joined by Agent N. Barry about 12:00 midnight.

Sometime around 1:00 AM, Barry and I observed a white Cadillac going north into the pick-up area. About 1:30 AM the group had not yet passed Dunlap and Henderson's position. As ample time had elapsed for the group to arrive at this point, Agents Gilbert and Bickley cut for sign on the trail about 2 miles South of Henderson and Dunlap and found the tracks still north bound.

We waited about another hour and I then instructed the officers to start tracking the group. Agents Dunlap and Henderson found tracks of the group going both north and south on the trail south on I-8. Agents Gilbert, Miller, Summers and Bickley picked up the tracks where they had crossed the freeway and back tracked the group to the pick-up area and joined Agent Barry and I. We followed the sign of the group to a point where we found the Cadillac, California license YOF 478, observed earlier. We found MILANES-Norfin, Felix lying in the front seat. He claimed to be a citizen of Mexico with no Immigration Documents. He also claimed he had no key to open the trunk of the vehicle. Gilbert opened a small hole behind the rear seat and observed what appeared to be bricks of marijuana in the trunk. Agent Miller produced a key to his personal automobile, which unlocked the trunk. It was stacked full of kilo bricks of marijuana. The subject was placed under arrest and advised of his rights. This was about 4:00 AM.

All eight Agents involved regrouped in Boulevard. While Agents Summers and Dunlap secured the Cadillac at Agent Lauborough's residence in Boulevard. Gilbert cut sign of the group farther south bound across hwy. 94. We took a secured panel and proceeded to the border in Jewell Valley arriving about 5 AM. On the way through Jewell Valley we had checked the North bound trail used by the group. At this point an accurate count of ten sets of tracks was obtained, by Agent Henderson. We hid the panel in the brush and secured the alien we had in custody. We went West and North back down the trail two or three hundred yards to a point where we felt sure the aliens would pass going South.

We then took-up positions in the brush along both sides of the trail and waited. Agent Summers and I were across from each other farthest North on the trail. Agents Gilbert and Miller were on the South end with the other four Agents in between us. Shortly before 6 AM we could hear the group coming toward us. It was still too dark to see without flashlights. As the first aliens in the group came between Summers and I Agent Barry stepped out and turned his light on the first subject in the group. Almost at the same instant I saw the flashes and heard the first subject fire three shots at Barry. As the other Agents returned the fire I saw more flashes and heard shots being fired from the group of aliens before they ran into the brush. I did not fire my revolver for fear of hitting Agent Summers who had been across the trail from me. As it turned out only three officers had a clear area to return the fire and did so, Agent Barry with his service revolver, Agent Gilbert using his service revolver and Agent Dunlap using a service issue shotgun.

The shooting only lasted a few seconds. When it was over Agent Barry had been hit in the back left shoulder area. Three aliens were laying in the road presumed dead and the rest were running through the brush.. Agents Gilbert and Miller were sent back to retrieve the panel and advise Chula Vista of the situation and that we were in need of assistance for Agent Barry. Agents Dunlap and Bickley drove Barry to a point farther North where a Coast Guard helicopter, requested by Chula Vista, could land and pick-up Barry to be taken to the hospital. Agents Henderson, Gilbert and I tracked the remaining seven aliens to the border fence.

Two Agents from the Drug Enforcement Agency, Button and Nickell, and two Tecate, B.C., Mex., police officers arrived South of the fence about 9:30 A.M. They had one person in custody, who they had apprehended walking South from the area. This person was also armed with a 22 caliber revolver. The subject had told the Agents that three of the aliens that had run South had been wounded. Only one weapon was found on the three dead aliens.

—A.W. Gordon

# Bob Gilbert Shooting

*Early 1970's, As told by Gordon Schneider (Retired)*

This incident occurred in Campo, CA station area in the early 1970's. Bob Gilbert (or Bob and a partner) one morning cut northbound tracks of five in an arroyo somewhere in Campo's rugged area of the border. The tracks went right down the middle of the sandy drainage Northward toward I-8. Bob got on them thinking it was nothing more than a tracking job for 5 wets. What he didn't know was that they had hauled weed to the highway and were coming back South on the same route.

Rounding a blind meander in the arroyo Bob found himself face to face with five mules, one of whom was pointing a pistol at him. He said he quickly drew his pistol and pointed it at them. I'm sure things happened fast at that point, faster than it takes to recount them. Bob said a mule tried to take his gun and he simply fired. I think that one was killed. Bob then fired on the one that was armed and wounded him. He then broke another's arm wrestling with him. The fourth one ran off and the fifth surrendered. Bob said he cuffed the one who surrendered to the wounded one, let the one with the broken arm walk on his own and they walked out leaving the body of the dead smuggler for later.

When he told me that story I said, "Jesus, Bob, they ought to clone you and put one of you in every vehicle for when the fizoo hits the fan". He looked at me and said kind of apologetically, "Yea, but I had a getaway". Now that's a Border Patrol Agent!

That aversion to shooting someone is a very real thing. I suspect it played a part in Bob Gilbert's 5 on 1 confrontation. If the smuggler with the gun is determined to shoot, then I don't see how Bob overcomes the odds like that. I figure the guy just held up the gun to intimidate Gilbert so they could get South. He never mentally committed to killing. Gilbert, on the other hand, was well programmed and well trained. The moment's hesitation was all he needed to seize the initiative.

## Gordon Schneider Incident

*As told by Gordon Schneider, PAIC, Eagle Pass, TX (Retired)*

The aversion to shoot someone is a very real thing. I first felt it back in Indio when I went to arrest a wet in broad daylight in a Coachella neighborhood. The wet took off running over fences and through yards with me right behind. I got him for the second time as he tried to scale a fence in a back yard. I grabbed him by the belt (in back) and the back of his shirt and pulled him off the fence. I then swung him in a circle and dumped him on the ground. He was on his back, I was sitting on top of him and the game should have been over (I thought). He was maybe 5'6" and 150 pounds. I'm 6'3" and 220 pounds. He's unarmed and I have a badge and a gun. It's all over.

It shocked me when he wouldn't stop struggling. I'm thinking I'm just going to give him a sandwich and a ride to Mexicali, what the hell is his deal? When I felt him reaching across my back with his right arm going for my gun my concern escalated and I punched him in the face, which opened a bloody cut over one eye. For just a moment he stopped fighting me and said something like "ay dios mio". I thought, O.K. he's done now, I'll cuff him and we're out of here.

Then he starts right back in again violently twisting, bridging and trying to get my gun. I didn't know it but I think my holster may have unsnapped when I was hopping fences in the beginning of the chase. The next thing I know, my gun is on the ground at my right side. I grab the handle, he grab's the barrel and cylinder. Blood is all over and felt like oil as I struggled to keep my grip and keep the gun pointed at him, it was a Smith Model 66.

It was at this point that it started to dawn on me that I was going to have to shoot this guy or he was going to shoot me. I remember there was a lady hanging laundry in the yard next to us. She was pinning things on the line and watching the struggle with total detachment. It seemed surreal. I couldn't believe I was going to have to shoot this guy. I started trigger pull just as my partner finally found us and ran up. Upon seeing the second agent, the guy gave up the fight.

I always envisioned a very different scenario when thinking about using deadly force. It was a clear-cut shoot situation against a real bad guy with a gun of his own and maybe a load of dope at night on the border. If the fellow I just arrested had been stronger or more skilled at fighting, I may not have kept control while my thought processes caught up with the situation, in other words, I was lucky.

# Loma Linda Ranch Episode

*Frank Arredondo Shooting, As told by Gordon Schneider, PAIC, Eagle Pass, TX (Retired)*

We'd had big marijuana loads come out of the Loma Linda area the whole three years I worked out of Eagle Pass. It was maybe 15 miles down river from Eagle Pass. At one point we got three one thousand pound loads within a two week span driving out of there. It was during the cold time of the year with freezing temperatures at night. I'm thinking it was late 1999 or early 2000 when we ran the operation that put Frank Arredondo in there.

We were going to cover that area covertly (guys in the bushes) and continuously for a week or two. SRT (Special Response Team) guys would go in for 72 hours at a time before being relieved by the next relay. Frank was set up near an aluminum gate they (Smugglers) always seemed to go through (Although they'd alternate between several different river landings). Another SRT Agent was laid in on another spot maybe 100 or 150 yards up river from Frank.

The incident occurred in the early morning hours just before Frank was to be extracted and relieved. He had not seen any activity the whole stretch. His walkie-talkie battery was low from being out so long. He heard the gate open and close and tried to count how many were passing through. It was very dark (no moon) and about freezing. His NVG's were no help as they fogged up in the cold. Frank wasn't sure, but thought maybe two or three wets had come by him and headed up the hill toward the lit ranch compound. He quickly decided to try to quietly follow them up the hill where he might silhouette them against the compound light. If they were just a few wets, as he suspected, he'd catch them and haul them out with him when he would be extracted, hopefully within the hour.

Frank started up the hill tactically. At one point he sensed something on the side of the trail and red lit it with the barrel-mounted flashlight.

Frank was armed with his .40 caliber pistol (Secondary) and a Colt M-4 (Primary). The long gun had a barrel mounted small flashlight with a flip up cover and red lens insert and a left hand activated pressure switch. Frank saw that what he lit were large white rocks next to the trail.

He then continued further up the trail until he said he just sensed someone there in front of him. His instincts told him to white light this time and he saw a suspect squatting maybe 25 feet in front of him near a mesquite tree. The guy had a short, riot type, pistol grip 12 gauge shotgun trained on Frank.

Frank told me he yelled right away for the guy to drop it. (The FBI and Texas Ranger, interestingly enough, later said the subject stated Frank told him something in English, which he claimed not to understand). To my way of thinking Frank was in a live or die situation where any commands were a risky waste of time. I also think there are situations where language becomes universal. A dope scout with a shotgun facing an agent with a .223 under those circumstances had to know that the agent's not asking him what time it is.

Frank had a whole series of thoughts that likely flashed in a micro-second. One of the first was recalling the pictures they showed him of close range shotgun wounds when he went through (F.I.T.P.) Firearms Instructor School. He figured that at that range it would be a fatal wound. He said he thought, "Is it a Gun", "Is it a Gun", yes, it's a gun.. Is it a real gun, yes it's a real gun. Frank told me he looked at the muzzle to be sure it was real. It looked huge he said. He yelled repeated commands for the guy to drop it without results. Frank flinched with his left hand a time or two briefly losing his light . The guy never lowered the muzzle but rather came up and forward slightly as if to fire. When the light blinked off, Frank said he had the thought that when he lit the light again he was going to have to fire. He did five times in semi-auto mode. One round hit the guy in the upper left thigh and took him down.

Frank quickly got the shotgun and asked where the others were. The suspect pointed out in the brush and Frank then dragged the guy into the clear roadway where the downed man and the others were on a single line in front of him. He said he could hear at least one breaking brush back toward the river. He then withdrew to brush cover performing a magazine exchange and pocketing the partly used magazine. Frank said the training he got from Rick Abbott (ITI Firearms Instructor and Ex-Seal) with the M-4 may have made the difference for him.

I was awakened by the phone and a radio operator saying an SRT guy had shot an alien—no more. I dressed and headed to the station and flew down to the scene by chopper with an A-Chief. I was never so glad to see a shotgun and find out the shooting was all, good. The scout got 9 ½ years in the joint (in addition to getting shot). He admitted he was hired to scout for a dope load but denied any intention of hurting anybody. Later when I returned to the scene it was daylight and I found a small baggie of marijuana near where the wounded fellow had been. He may have been stoned when he came across the river.

Frank said it looked to him like the guy was trying to fire but couldn't make it happen for some reason (Safety on?). He admitted he was given the shotgun right before crossing and was unfamiliar with it. If the bad guy was determined and competent Frank would likely have died. It's possible the guy just succumbed to the natural human aversion to shooting another human being. Just locked up long enough for Frank to get his shots off first. That aversion to shooting someone is a very real thing.

—Gordon Schneider (Retired)

# A Tale of the Tiger

*By Jerry Edmison*

The Chamizal Treaty of 1963 settled a century-old dispute between the U.S. and Mexico over a 600-acre parcel of land near El Paso, Texas that Mexico claimed belonged to them ostensibly because of a shift in the river during a flood after the Treaty of Guadalupe Hidalgo in 1848 had defined the Rio Grande River as a boundary between the two countries. Presidents, John F. Kennedy and Adolfo Lopez Mateos signed the Treaty, whereby the U.S. Ceded the sliver of land back to Mexico, and a Memorial at the site now commemorates that peaceful territorial transfer.

I arrived in El Paso on January 3rd, 1966 and was sworn-in along with four other Border Patrol Inspector trainees, and after graduating from the Border Patrol Academy in Port Isabel, Texas, returned to El Paso to begin a career that spanned the better part of four decades. The entire complement of Patrolmen of the El Paso Border Patrol Station was tasked by the terms of the treaty to continue to control the area defined by the settlement and regard it as U.S. territory until the new river channel could be excavated. Several hundred families and businesses had to be relocated, buildings razed, and two new international bridges and ports of entry had to be reconstructed. It was amid the conditions of this chaotic backdrop that my hands-on practical training was to commence, yet I was more than eager to put into practice the knowledge and pent-up energy that 4 months in a classroom environment can generate.

This was the era when the Vietnam War was beginning to heat up, and the Johnson Administration had opted for "guns" instead of "butter", which placed the INS far down on the federal appropriations list. Our car radios were WWII vintage and Journeyman Patrol Inspectors had to furnish almost everything in the performance of their duties such as ear and eye protection during pistol qualifications, as well as their own uniforms, which included gold chain-type tie clasps that were very expensive and difficult to acquire since few retail stores maintained those antiquated accouterments in stock.

It seemed that almost every patrolman at the El Paso Station had a nickname, and it did not take long for the station's venerable raconteur and moniker giver- Glen "Punchy" Painter – to bestow each of us with the handles that would follow us throughout our careers. For example: there was Frank "Whip" Wilson; Charles "Fireplug" Wernette; and Barry "the Boy Wonder" Jackson, but Punchy, for some reason, shelved the donning of my nickname until he could size me up a bit.

South El Paso has always been a dangerous place to work. Thirty-six years and 100 lbs. ago my enthusiasm for the job seemed to frequently find me in situations where physical confrontations and altercations were the order of the day, and with that in mind, Punchy decided to dub me "El Tigre". Although many officers were not particularly fond of their unsolicited nicknames, I bore mine with a considerable amount of pride. The Tiger became sort of my own personal totem, but "pride", being the first of the seven deadly sins, would soon lead me precariously into harms way, where only a twist of fate would ultimately save my life.

Ray Barrios and I were working an evening shift late one fall afternoon and were assigned to the area around the Santa Fe Street Port of Entry and bridge area. The Port had a cubicle on the roof of the building that we called the "tower" which afforded an officer a lofty unrestricted view of the border for a mile or so both upriver and downriver. We were in position that day to respond to any illegal entries that the officer observed, and had been watching the demolition of Old Camp Chigas, which was the original El Paso Sector Headquarters where my father had entered on duty as a Patrol Inspector in 1941. A sense of sadness came over me as I watched the bulldozers plow thoughtlessly through the two-story brick compound. The new river channel was slated to pass right through that area.

Anyone who worked the tower was in a position to observe the many Mexican street urchins who used the cover of the bridge as a sort of home base for their forays into downtown Juarez and El Paso where they begged, robbed, snatched purses-intermittently sniffing glue that they would steal, or that would be sold to them by their elders. Generations of these children had honed their skills at petty criminal pursuits and most had grown up to commit more serious crimes as adults. They were a constant pain in the rear, but had to be dealt with on a daily basis. The Mexican Police would always shear the heads of juveniles that they encountered committing crimes in Juarez, which made it easier for them to be recognized on the street.

If memory serves me correctly, "Bull Moose" Morris was working the tower that day and radioed us that a pair of male juveniles with sheared heads, who appeared to be around 17 or 18 years old, was running from the police down Avenida Juarez towards the river. They were dressed in blue denim shirts and blue jeans, which suggested that they had escaped from incarceration somewhere in Mexico. Ray responded, "…keep us advised where they are likely to cross the river."

"Ten-four", he said.

A few minutes later Bull Moose came on the air again. "They are going to hit the river about two hundred yards upriver from the Santa Fe bridge, and it looks like the police have broken off the chase."

Ray was driving that day and the sedan was facing downriver. He started to turn the vehicle around to be in position to spot the duo when they emerged from the river bottom when I brashly volunteered to go after the pair on foot. They had waded the river at a place where the water was about waist deep and were headed towards the levee and a cluster of old tenement buildings. I started running to head them off and was up to full speed when I hung the toe of my boot on a green Tumble Weed, and tumble I did, doing a complete somersault, landing spread eagle on the ground.

There was nothing hurt but my pride, but the pair had seen my rather flamboyant non-acrobatic plunge and had retreated back to the river. There was no way now that I could let them escape. As they ambled back into the water with their backs toward me, thinking that the chase was over, I dove off a small embankment, grabbing each with a headlock on my way down. When we all surfaced the larger fellow whose head I was grasping with my left arm, began fighting me, and grabbed my tie, which luckily was a snap-on type. When he realized that he would be unable to choke me, he threw the tie into the water. The shorter lad on my right side was not struggling, so most of my attention was directed toward this lively opponent who was becoming harder and harder to control with one arm.

It was at that point that a strange feeling came over me, and when I looked down at my other side, the shorter individual had unsnapped my pistol from the holster and was pointing it at the right side of my abdomen, trying to cock back the hammer. I pushed the more combative youth away and wrestled my pistol back from this new menace. Ray arrived on the riverbank about that time, so I handcuffed him and was attempting to hand him up to where Ray could place him into the patrol car, when a large piece of broken concrete landed on the embankment a few feet from my head. My former combatant had made it back to a sandbar and began throwing anything that would serve as a projectile in my direction. As Ray was dragging the other writhing alien by the handcuffs back towards the patrol car, another piece of concrete landed in my vicinity. As I was floundering around in the mud trying to gain high ground, Ray pulled out his .357 Magnum and yelled at the young adult to stop throwing things, and when he didn't, Ray fired a round near his feet, which ricocheted up in the air toward the vicinity of a retaining wall on the Mexican side. About a dozen or so individuals who were sitting on the wall watching the goings-on began scurrying towards cover after the bullet whizzed over their heads.

A group of locals on our side of the river began gathering near our vehicle, and as I was about to top the berm, I heard several individuals in a rather pitiful tones of voice say, *"Pobrecita."* I raced the translation through my mind: *Now let's see, Pobre means Poor, and anything with an ITA or ITO means something small or diminutive, and a noun must agree in number and gender. An O ending means male and an A means ...Uh Oh....I knew that they were not talking about me.*

Ray's attention had been, and continued to be drawn toward the threat in the river bottom, and had not noticed that the arrested youth's jeans were now around the thigh area, and there was no doubt now that the *He* who had attempted to shoot me was really a *she*.

"Oh hell Tiger," Ray said frantically, "Pull her pants back up...we don't need an international incident here." I thought to myself: *this incident may be nothing compared to the possible repercussions that an errant bullet fired into the sovereign Republic of Mexico might create, depending upon where it had lodged itself.*

Well, the "Poor Little One" now had an audience, and she made the most of it. I have attempted some very challenging things in my time, but trying to pull up a pair of skintight wet blue jeans on a female who was screaming and kicking me in the shins, has to rate among the most difficult. Bull Moose had radioed Senior Patrol Inspector Davidson to assist us, and he arrived on the scene and volunteered to take her off our hands, write her up and V/R her back to Mexico. He had not witnessed the entire incident and had no idea what he was letting himself in for.

As night fell and my adrenalin level began to subside, I took everything out of my wallet and laid it on the hood of the sedan to dry. I couldn't erase the mental picture of my tie, and $20 gold plated tie clasp, floating down the river, never to be seen again. Then a chill ran down my spine as I pondered what my epitaph might have been had fate not intervened: *Here lies El Tigre, taken in the prime of life at the hands of two glue-sniffing illegal aliens. Foolish Pride would not allow him to simply chase them back across the border. RIP.*

Bull Moose came back on the radio. "That was quite a rodeo Tigre. Be advised that SPI Davidson is V/Ring her back to Mexico right now and she is trying to kick out the back window of his vehicle. I guess I was wrong about those two being males."

"Ten-four" I said, "so was I."

Many things have changed since that unforgettable day. The U. S. Border Patrol is now the best-equipped agency in the country, sidearm holsters are much more secure, and Agents, as they are called now, are no longer required to wear those god-awful ties with rough duty uniforms. Every piece of equipment is now state of the art and funding seems to be the least of the agency's worries. **Operation Hold the Line** has finally resolved the criminal alien problem in El Paso.

Every time that my wife and I travel through El Paso towards Deming, New Mexico to visit our son and daughter-in-law, both of whom are Border Patrol Agents there, I look off I-10 towards the site of the incident, which is now part of Juarez, and reflect upon the close call of that fateful day. I also think about Ray Barrios, who stuck his neck out for a young inexperienced officer by firing a "warning shot", which everyone knows is against regulations, but gratefully negated the threat to my welfare. But mostly, I thank my lucky stars that the bellicose young woman who had grabbed my pistol was unaware that simply pulling the trigger of my sidearm would have fired the weapon. Her lack of knowledge of double actions on modern side arms had given me the split second opportunity to quell the shooting. I guess that it was just not my time to go.

They were all lessons well learned and have served me positively over the years in other dangerous situations.

—Jerry Edmison

# Shooting Incident Vega Verde Area

*David Toothman, SRT Leader, Del Rio Sector Special Response Team, January 14, 2003*

Our team received information at 1600 hours from the Del Rio Sector Intelligence office concerning a half ton of marijuana that was supposed to cross the Rio Grande in the Del Rio area at approximately 1930 hours. We received permission to work the traffic at around 1800 hours.

The information was very specific. We were informed that a local branch of the "bloods" gang, were renting a house on the Rio Grande River near Lake Amistad Dam. The house is located approximately 50 yards from the river.

At around 1900 hours the gang members living in the house would depart their car and leave the gate to their property open. At approximately 1915 hours three cars would drive into the property and behind the house (in between the river and the house) and close the gate behind them. At around 1930 hours "mules" from Mexico would cross a half-ton of marijuana and load it into the waiting cars which would then leave. About 30 minutes later the renters would return and be able to deny any knowledge of what had just occurred on their property.

At 1800 hours we deployed a three-man team, one armed with an M-4, and the other two with .40 pistols to the area and they infiltrated in by foot taking extra precaution not to be seen. At 1900 hours the renters left. At 1930 the three load vehicles drove in and closed the gate and our agents spotted several rafts with large piles of marijuana crossing just upriver of their position.

At this time myself and five other agents (all armed with M-4's) were about three miles away in a vehicle. We were going to infiltrate and watch three positions just down river of where this was all taking place, just to make sure we did not lose the marijuana. Once we heard the radio traffic from our team on the ground we began making our way towards them. Our three-man team waited until the smugglers had loaded several of the marijuana bundles into the vehicles and then "jumped" the load.

As soon as they did this, all of the mules and the three car drivers ran and jumped into the river. Once they were in the river automatic gunfire erupted from the Mexican shoreline. Intelligence gathered from different enforcement sources (that has been since verified several times) to us that there were twelve Mexican Federal Judicial Police armed with M-16's firing at our team. It turns out that these guys "protect and escort" drug loads that cross into the United States in this particular area. Our agents returned fire and had to move back to an area of better coverage due to the volume and accuracy of the Mexican fire.

The fire-fight lasted for around 5 to 10 minutes and a total of about 1000 rounds were exchanged (our guys shot around 25 rounds). Within a minute of the end of the shooting, myself and five others pulled up and ran over to assist the ground team. We moved back to the river while redistributing ammunition (the three original agents were all out of ammo). We found two United States Citizens (teenage "bloods") and 1100 pounds of marijuana. The gang bangers were arrested, three cars, one house, and 1100 pounds of marijuana seized. The third car driver turned himself in 2 days later.

Once again intelligence from the other law enforcement sources told later that our guys killed three of the Mexican gunmen and shot ones ear off hospitalizing him. Not a peep came out of Mexico about the shooting. No radio or new reports, which is highly unusual. We believe this is due to the involvement of the Mexican Federal Judicial Police. There have been rumors that the "bloods" are trying to purchase ballistic body armor and Kevlar helmets but we believe this to be nothing but false bravado and a Kevlar vest won't stop .223 anyway.

—David Toothman
SRT Team Leader

# The Life of a U.S. Border Patrol Agent

## DAY-TO-DAY OPERATIONS

1. The Prevention and Apprehension of Illegal Aliens

2. Drug Seizures

The following pictures show marijuana seized during daily activity of U.S. Border Patrol Agents, Eagle Pass, Texas
—Jim And Delores Gregg

*Fig. 90. Eagle Pass Border Patrol Station, 2021 pounds of marijuana found hidden in the frame of the stock trailer shown on the next page (02-02-00)*

Fig. 91. Marijuana shown on the preceding page, was hidden on the lower frame of this stock trailer. For cover the smuggler carried a load of goats. DEA got the dope, a rancher got the goats and U.S.B.P. got the truck, trailer and its driver. Eagle Pass Border Patrol Station.

Fig. 92. Border Patrol Agents apprehend 7887.15 pounds of marijuana, Eagle Pass, Texas, February 25, 1996 (Courtesy Rudy Rodriguez U.S.B.P.)

196 + THE GREGG METHOD OF FIRE CONTROL

Fig. 93. U.S.B.P. Agent, Rudy Rodriguez, with the above load of marijuana, street value $6,300.000.00 (Courtesy Rudy Rodriguez U.S.B.P.)

Fig. 94. A Nights Work

*Fig. 95. A Days Work (Courtesy Rudy Rodriguez U.S.B.P.)*

*Fig. 96. Fort Hancock, Texas U.S. Border Patrol Station, 577.11 pounds of Marijuana, January 28, 1997*

*Fig. 97. David Justice (Left), Rudy Rodriguez and Gary Bear on the shore of the Rio Grande River, just waiting for transportation (Courtesy Rudy Rodriguez)*

198 + THE GREGG METHOD OF FIRE CONTROL

## A Drug Bust in Action

Agents attach a winch to the vehicle and pull it to shore.

*Fig. 98. An almost new Chevrolet Suburban was used to move a load of marijuana across the Rio Grande River into the U.S. When the smugglers spotted Border Patrol Agents they attempted to make it back to Mexico but the vehicle got stuck, the smugglers bailed out and made it back to Mexico. (Courtesy Joe Tammen, U.S.B.P. Fort Hancock, TX)*

*Fig. 99. Off loading Marijuana (Courtesy Joe Tammen U.S.B.P.)*

Fig. 100. The vehicle becomes government property. (Courtesy Joe Tammen, U.S.B.P.)

Fig. 101. The DEA and the incinerator will get the dope! (Courtesy Joe Tammen, U.S.B.P.)

Fig. 102. Gordon Schneider (Left), Frank Arredondo (Back) and Angel Rivera canoeing the Rio Grande in a driving rain down river from Del Rio, Texas. G.P.S., S. R. T. Operation Alien Landing/Crossings on the Rio Grande River. (07-23-97) (Courtesy Gordon Schneider)

Fig. 103. Frank Arredondo (rear) and Angel Rivera canoeing the Rio Grande river on an S.R.T. Operation. "Lonesome Dove" movie set in the background on the Moody Ranch down river from Del Rio, Texas

Fig 104. This picture was taken upriver from Langtree, Texas while sign-cutting along the Rio Grand River. Gordon Schneider (above) and another agent found the dead Gar fish. Gordon said "It was longer than my arm span (6'3") and had to weigh 100 pounds. (Courtesy Gordon Schneider)

# Jim Gregg's Shooting School

"Hole in One Club"
Membership

## "Hole-In-One Club"

In February 1991, Jim Gregg's Shooting School formally established a "Hole-In-One Club". This gives recognition to those handgun shooters who shoot five bullets, all touching, at a distance of 15 feet, without the use of sights.

An analysis of the training classes show that 85 to 100% of all students join the "Hole-In-One Club". This is normally accomplished during the first 150 bullets fired.

Fig. 105. David K. LaMascus U.S.B.P., Uvalde, Texas 02-23-98

# Hole-In-One Members

## As of February 14, 2004

| Name | Organization | Year |
|---|---|---|
| Abrams, Jeff | USBP Nogales, AZ | 2002 |
| Acosta, Gabriel H. | USBP Laredo, TX | 1999 |
| Acosta, Juan L. | USBP Laredo South, TX | 2000 |
| Acosta, Samuel | USBP Carrizo Springs, TX | 2001 |
| Acosta, Victor | USBP Brackettville, TX | 2000 |
| Acuna, Edward | USBP Eagle Pass, TX | 1997/00 |
| Adam, Philip L. | USBP Port Angeles, WA | 1994 |
| Adams, Terry | Burlington Northern R.R. | 1993 |
| Adams, Zachary | Pasadena, California | 2004 |
| Aguirre, Richard | USBP Eagle Pass, TX | 2001 |
| Akeroyd, Chuck | USBP Del Rio, TX | 2000 |
| Akin, Larry D. | El Paso County S/O, TX | 1993 |
| Alamillo, Jose Luis | USBP Brackettville, TX | 2000 |
| Alaniz, Daniel | USBP Laredo North, TX | 2000 |
| Alaniz, Marcelino, Jr. | US/INS San Antonio, TX | 2003 |
| Alatorre, Reynaldo | USBP Laredo North, TX | 2000 |
| Alcaraz, Armando | USBP Del Rio, TX | 1997 |
| Aldaco, Roberto, Jr. | USBP Del Rio, TX | 1998 |
| Allen, Jim | INS Seattle, WA | 1991 |
| Alonso, Juan | USBP Eagle Pass, TX | 1997/00/01 |
| Alva, Estevan | USBP Laredo South, TX | 2000 |
| Ames, Danny H. | Stillwater County S/O, MT | 1996 |
| Amster, Howard Scott | USBP Brownsville, TX | 1993 |
| Anaya, Domingo | USBP Laredo North, TX | 2000 |
| Anderson, Daryl | Renewable Resources, Yukon | 1994 |
| Anderson, Mark | Montana. Fish, Wildlife & Parks, MT | 1996 |
| Anderson, Mark D. | US Customs-Air San Angelo, TX | 1993 |

| | | |
|---|---|---|
| Anderson, Pamela M. | USBP Laredo North, TX | 1993 |
| Andrade, Daniel | USBP Del Rio, TX | 1997 |
| Aponte, Hector I. | USBP Eagle Pass, TX | 1999 |
| Arce, David M. | USBP Carrizo Springs, TX | 1997 |
| Arguello, Andrew | USBP Laredo South, TX | 1999/00 |
| Arechiga, Jose L. | USBP Comstock, TX | 2001 |
| Armstrong, James | USBP Eagle Pass, TX | 1999 |
| Arnold, Donald | USBP Del Rio, TX | 1997 |
| Arnold, William, Jr. | USBP Uvalde, TX | 1998 |
| Arredondo, Francisco | USBP Brackettville, TX | 1997 |
| Ashford, Whitney A. | USBP Laredo North, TX | 2000 |
| Ashlaw, Richard L. | USBP Del Rio, TX | 1993 |
| Aukland, Richard T. | USBP Bismark, ND | 1994 |
| Avila, Adrian B. | USBP Del Rio, TX | 2000 |
| Babb, Benjamin | USBP Comstock, TX | 1998 |
| Babbey, Steve A. | USBP Del Rio, TX | 1998 |
| Baer. Gary D. | USBP Eagle Pass, TX | 1997 |
| Baggett, Byron P. | USBP Eagle Pass, TX | 2001 |
| Bagocus, Jack | USBP Lynden, WA | 1994 |
| Bailey, James T. | USBP Brackettville, TX | 1998 |
| Bailey, Matthew T. | USBP Eagle Pass, TX | 1999 |
| Baird, Kenneth V. | USBP Bellingham, WA | 1994 |
| Baker, Derek S. | USBP Eagle Pass, TX | 1999 |
| Baker, Scott | USBP Twin Falls, ID | 1994 |
| Baker, William B. | US Customs-Air San Antonio, TX | 1993 |
| Bakos, Jason J. | USBP Laredo South, TX | 2000 |
| Bakowski, Robert V. | USBP Trenton, MI | 1994 |
| Balchuck, Derek | USBP Del Rio, TX | 1997 |
| Ballard, Rowdy | USBP Hebbronville, TX | 1999 |
| Ballinger, Noel G. | Royal City P.D., WA | 1991 |
| Banda, Jesus D. | USBP Brackettville, TX | 2000 |
| Banda, Rodolfo | USBP Eagle Pass, TX | 1997 |
| Banks, Jim | FLETC Artesia, NM | 1998 |
| Barber, Vernon W. | US Customs-Air San Antonio, TX | 1993 |
| Barbery, Harry C. | USBP Brackettville, TX | 1998 |
| Barger, Douglas | Grant County S/O, Ephrata, WA | 1999 |

| | | |
|---|---|---|
| Barnes, Britt A. | USBP Eagle Pass, TX | 1992/97 |
| Barnett, Michael | Montana State Prison, MT | 1997 |
| Barniol, Luis M. | USBP Spokane, WA | 1993 |
| Baron, Alfred N. | US/INS Eagle, Pass, TX | 2003 |
| Barrera, Arturo | USBP Eagle Pass, TX | 1997 |
| Barrera, Rodolfo, Jr. | USBP Zapata, TX | 1999 |
| Barrett, Edward M. | USBP Ysleta, TX | 1992 |
| Barrow, Morris L. | USBP Eagle Pass, TX | 1999 |
| Bassett, Griff | USBP Plentywood, MT | 1994 |
| Bauman, Alvin F. | USBP Oroville, WA | 1993 |
| Baumann, James W. | USBP Duluth, MI | 1994 |
| Baumgardner, Jan B. | US/INS San Antonio, TX | 2003 |
| Baxter, George | USBP Eagle Pass, TX | 1997 |
| Beach, James C. | USBP Eagle Pass, TX | 1999 |
| Beams, Tracy | USBP Del Rio, TX | 2000 |
| Beard, James P. | US/INS San Antonio, TX | 2003 |
| Beardy, Peter | RCMP Whitehorse, Yukon | 1995 |
| Beattie, Ray F. | USBP El Paso, TX | 1991 |
| Beets, Scotty W. | USBP Eagle Pass, TX | 1999 |
| Bell, Franklin E. | FLETC Artesia, NM | 1998 |
| Bell, Jon M. | USBP Uvalde, TX | 2001 |
| Beltran, Daniel | Fire Marshal El Paso, TX | 1993 |
| Benavides, Joe N. | US/INS San Antonio, TX | 2003 |
| Benavides, Juan M. | USBP Eagle Pass, TX | 1999 |
| Bennett, Dean J. | Great Falls P.D., MT | 1996 |
| Bennett, Matthew L. | USBP Carrizo Springs, TX | 1997 |
| Benton, Donna J. | USBP Eagle Pass, TX | 1999 |
| Berny, Thomas E. | US/INS Del Rio, TX | 2003 |
| Beza, Beau | USBP Carrizo Springs, TX | 2001 |
| Biallas, Mark | Grant County S/O, Ephrata, WA | 2002 |
| Biggins, Tracy | USBP Del Rio, TX | 2000 |
| Billings, Eric A. | USBP Eagle Pass, TX | 1999/01 |
| Bilyk, Greg A. | USBP Eagle Pass, TX | 2001 |
| Bippley, Chris | USBP Sierra Blanca, TX | 1991 |
| Bjerkelund, David B. | USBP Laredo North, TX | 2000 |
| Black, Hector | USBP Eagle Pass, TX | 1997 |

| | | |
|---|---|---|
| Black, Jake | USBP Lynden, WA | 1994 |
| Blackwell, David E. | US Customs-Air San Antonio, TX | 1993 |
| Blais, Alexander F. | USBP Del Rio, TX | 2000 |
| Blake, Brian | USBP Del Rio, TX | 1998 |
| Blanks, Gerald L. | USBP Fresno, CA | 1991 |
| Blaz, Thomas D. | Montana State Prison, MT | 1997 |
| Blinner, James E., Jr. | USBP Whitefish, MT | 2001 |
| Bocanegra, Jose L. | USBP Carrizo Springs, TX | 2001 |
| Bodnar, David R. | USBP Uvalde, TX | 2001 |
| Boehrns, Bruce W. | USBP Bottineau, ND | 1994 |
| Bonner, Victor R. | USBP Brackettville, TX | 1998 |
| Bonbright, Robert | USBP Blaine, WA | 1994 |
| Bordovsky, John, IV | USBP Uvalde, TX | 1998 |
| Boris, John | US/INS San Antonio, TX | 2003 |
| Borries, Bob D. | Burlington Northern R.R. | 1993 |
| Bosch, Miguel | USBP Eagle Pass, TX | 1999 |
| Botello, Pedro | USBP Uvalde, TX | 2001 |
| Bourgeois, Jack E. | Lafayette Parrish S/O, LA | 1991 |
| Bowers, Kevin L. | Renewable Resources, Yukon | 1995 |
| Bowman, John F. | USBP Eagle Pass, TX | 1992/97 |
| Bowman, Stephen D. | USBP Laredo South, TX | 2000 |
| Boylan, Michael J. | US Marshal Seattle, WA | 1996 |
| Bradford, Keith A. | USBP Eagle Pass, TX | 1999 |
| Braesicke, Dudley | USBP Brackettville, TX | 1998 |
| Bragg, R. Eric | USBP Comstock, TX | 2001 |
| Brandt, Nolan R. | USBP Del Rio, TX | 1998 |
| Brashear, Kevin P. | USBP Carrizo Springs, TX | 1992/97 |
| Brennan, Paul M. | USBP Uvalde, TX | 1998 |
| Briggs, Larry | Montana State Prison, MT | 1998 |
| Brinson, Danny M. | USBP Port Angeles, WA | 1994 |
| Brown, Patrick A. | USBP Fort Hancock, TX | 1997 |
| Brown, Phillip S. | USBP Eagle Pass, TX | 1999 |
| Brown, Samuel D. | USBP Laredo North, TX | 2000 |
| Brugman, Gary M. | USBP Eagle Pass, TX | 1999 |
| Bryan, Lyle P. | USBP Spokane, WA | 1993/01 |
| Bryan, Russell | Burlington Northern R.R. | 1993 |

| | | |
|---|---|---|
| Bucher, Jeremy M. | USBP Ajo, AZ | 2002 |
| Budd, Greg | Montana State Prison, MT | 1998 |
| Buentello, Matias, Jr. | USBP Carrizo Springs, TX | 1997 |
| Bullard, Clyde, Jr. | USBP Carrizo Springs, TX | 1997 |
| Bunting, James R. | USBP Eagle Pass, TX | 1997 |
| Burdette, James A. | USBP Laredo, TX | 1999 |
| Burditt, Darryl | Conrad P.D., MT | 1996 |
| Burgin, Kevin D. | USBP Eagle Pass, TX | 1997 |
| Burns, Todd D. | USBP Carrizo Springs, TX | 1997 |
| Busby, David L. | USBP Del Rio, TX | 1997 |
| Bush, John A. | USBP Eagle Pass, TX | 1999 |
| Cabellero, Andres | USBP Comstock, TX | 1998 |
| Camacho, Marco | USBP Brackettville, TX | 2001 |
| Campisi, Leah D. | US Customs-Air San Angelo, TX | 1993 |
| Cano, Edgar P. | USBP Eagle Pass, TX | 1997 |
| Canterbury, Rick M. | Grant County S/O, WA | 1993 |
| Cantu, Christopher T. | USBP Laredo, TX | 1999 |
| Cantu, Amancio, Jr. | US/INS San Antonio, TX | 2003 |
| Cantu, Felix, Jr. | USBP Del Rio, TX | 1993/97 |
| Cantu, Francisco, Jr. | USBP Rocksprings, TX | 1998 |
| Cantu, Gustavo | USBP Brackettville, TX | 1998 |
| Cantu, Juan J. | USBP Eagle Pass, TX | 1999 |
| Cantu, Mario, Jr. | USBP Carrizo Springs, TX | 1997 |
| Cantu, Raymundo, Jr. | US/INS Laredo, TX | 2003 |
| Cantu, Noel | USBP Hebbronville, TX | 1999 |
| Cardona, Orlando | USBP Eagle Pass, TX | 2001 |
| Carlile, Keith | Grant County S/O, WA | 1993/96 |
| Carlson, Charles E. | Grant County S/O, WA | 1993 |
| Carlson, Glenn L. | USBP Shelby, MT | 1994 |
| Carlson, Steven M. | US Customs-Air San Angelo, TX | 1993 |
| Carnevale, Americo B. | INS Seattle, WA | 1993 |
| Carpenter, Douglas A. | USBP Billings, MT | 1994 |
| Carrasco, Rene' | USBP Del Rio, TX | 1998 |
| Carruthers, William E. | Burlington Northern R.R. | 1993 |
| Casas, Luckey | USBP Eagle Pass, TX | 1997 |
| Cason, Roy D. | USBP Pecos, TX | 1993 |

| | | |
|---|---|---|
| Cass, William R. | USBP Carrizo Springs, TX | 1997 |
| Castelar, Jaime | USBP Del Rio, TX | 1998 |
| Castillo, Jose L. | USBP Del Rio, TX | 2000 |
| Castleberry, Willie | USBP San Angelo, TX | 1992 |
| Castloo, Thomas | USBP Comstock, TX | 1998 |
| Castro, Alberto, Jr. | USBP Laredo South, TX | 2000 |
| Cathel, Jeff | Great Falls P.D., MT | 1997 |
| Cauraugh, Mike W. | Contra County S/O, CA | 1991 |
| Cavazos, George Jr. | USBP Brackettville, TX | 2001 |
| Cavazos, Jose | USBP Laredo South, TX | 2000 |
| Cavazos, Marco A. | USBP Carrizo Springs, TX | 2000 |
| Celano, Michael A. | USBP Detroit, MI | 1994 |
| Cerda, Orlando | USBP Comstock, TX | 1997 |
| Cervantes, Enrique | USBP Carrizo Springs, TX | 2000 |
| Cervantes, Marco A. | USBP Eagle Pass, TX | 1999 |
| Chambless, David R. | USBP Carrizo Springs, TX | 2001 |
| Chan, Jesus A. | USBP Laredo South, TX | 2000 |
| Chandler, William | USBP Del Rio, TX | 1998 |
| Chang, Henry II | USBP Laredo South, TX | 2000 |
| Chaseperry, Ryan | USBP Carrizo Springs, TX | 2001 |
| Chavez, Tomas, Jr. | USBP Laredo North, TX | 2000 |
| Chavira, Norberto | USBP Comstock, TX | 2001 |
| Chong, Federico Jr. | USBP Carrizo Springs, TX | 2001 |
| Christensen, Alan C. | USBP Blaine, WA | 1994 |
| Christensen, Richard | Stillwater County S/O, MT | 1996 |
| Ciseros, Enrique, Jr. | USBP Laredo North, TX | 2000 |
| Clanahan, Steven L. | USBP Carrizo Springs, TX | 1992/97 |
| Clark, Martin R. | USBP Eagle Pass, TX | 1999 |
| Clarke, Sheppard | Tacoma P.D., WA | 1996 |
| Clawson, Chuck | Montana State Prison, MT | 1997/98 |
| Clem, Chris T. | USBP Lordsburg, NM | 2003 |
| Clough, George A. | Montana Dept. Of Corrections, Libby, MT | 1998 |
| Coates, Gregory L. | US Customs-Air San Antonio, TX | 1993 |
| Coe, Brad | USBP Brackettville, TX | 1998 |
| Coleman, Billy Lee, Jr. | USBP Eagle Pass, TX | 1999 |
| Coleman, Jason E. | Montana State Prison, MT | 1997/98 |

| | | |
|---|---|---|
| Collins, Eric J., II | Burlington Northern R.R. | 1993 |
| Collins, Louis W. | USBP Laredo North, TX | 2000 |
| Colman, Ramon | USBP Abilene, TX | 1998 |
| Condon, Joseph M. | US Customs-Air San Angelo, TX | 1993 |
| Connors, Mikeal J. | USBP Sonoita, AZ | 2002 |
| Conteras, Hector | USBP Carrizo Springs, TX | 1997 |
| Contreras, Salvador | USBP Del Rio, TX | 2001 |
| Conway, Danny J. | USBP El Paso, TX | 1991 |
| Cook, James E. | INS Seattle, WA | 1991 |
| Cook, Kim W. | Grant County S/O, WA | 1993/99 |
| Cook, Randy D. | USBP Carrizo Springs, TX | 1997 |
| Cooper, Ron | FLETC Artesia, NM | 1998 |
| Cooper, Ronald K. | U.S.B.P. Del Rio, TX | 2001 |
| Cormier, Robert G. | Lafayette Marshal Office, LA | 1991 |
| Cornehl, Brian W. | USBP Wenatchee, WA | 2001 |
| Corp, David Eugene | USBP Del Rio, TX | 2000 |
| Courtney, Charles | US/INS San Antonio, TX | 2003 |
| Courtney, Charles K. | USBP Brackettville, TX | 1998 |
| Cox, Daniel | USBP Eagle Pass, TX | 1999 |
| Cox, James B. | USBP Laredo North, TX | 2000 |
| Coxarrubias, David | USBP Uvalde, TX | 2001 |
| Cravey, James | USBP Laredo South, TX | 2000 |
| Crawford, James W. | USBP Port Huron, MI | 1994 |
| Cronen, C.M. | US/INS Laredo, TX | 2003 |
| Crosby, Tom | USBP Spokane, WA | 1993 |
| Cross, Rick D. | USBP Del Rio, TX | 1997 |
| Crouse, Sonny | USBP Las Cruces, NM | 1991 |
| Croy, Emmett E. | USBP Del Rio, TX | 1998 |
| Cruz, Albert H., Jr. | US/INS San Antonio, TX | 2003 |
| Cruz, Mary Jane G. | USBP El Paso, TX | 1991 |
| Cruz, Ramiro | USBP Uvalde, TX | 1998 |
| Culpepper, Richard | US/INS San Antonio, TX | 2003 |
| Cunningham, Curtis | USBP El Paso, TX | 1991 |
| Curbow, Sean D. | USBP Laredo North, TX | 2000 |
| Curiel, Felipe | USBP Del Rio, TX | 1997 |
| Curtis, Franklin S. Jr. | USBP Uvalde, TX | 2001 |

| | | |
|---|---|---|
| Czechowicz, Bradley | USBP Carrizo Springs, TX | 2000 |
| Czechowicz, Kevin J. | USBP Del Rio, TX | 2000 |
| Dahlstrom, M. Blaine | INS Spokane, WA | 1991 |
| Dale, Tim | USBP Del Rio, TX | 2000 |
| Danson, Bruce R. | USBP Del Rio, TX | 2000 |
| Daniels, Bill R. | USBP El Paso, TX | 1992 |
| Daugherty, Ian | USBP Laredo South, TX | 2000 |
| Davidson, William E. | FLETC Artesia, NM | 1998 |
| Davila, Antonio | USBP Eagle Pass, TX | 2000 |
| Davis, Gary K. | USBP Eagle Pass, TX | 1999/00 |
| Davis, Gene | USBP Blaine, WA | 1994 |
| Deanda, Richard Jr. | USBP Nogales, AZ | 2002 |
| Deason, Thomas G. | USBP St. Mary, MT | 1994 |
| Debruhl, Michael R. | USBP Carrizo Springs, TX | 1992 |
| Degrenia, Mark R. | USBP Del Rio, TX | 1997 |
| Deimel, Robert G. | USBP Eagle Pass, TX | 1997 |
| Delagarza, Jesus M. | US/INS Laredo, TX | 2003 |
| Delarosa, David | USBP Hebbronville, TX | 1999 |
| De La Torre, Ruben | USBP Uvalde, TX | 2000 |
| Deleon, Alberto A. | USBP Laredo South, TX | 2000 |
| Deleon, Alexander W. | USBP Carrizo Springs, TX | 1992/97/00 |
| Deleon, Jose, Jr. | US/INS San Antonio, TX | 2003 |
| Deleon, Luis L. | USBP Laredo, TX | 1999 |
| Delgado, Danny | USBP Ysleta, TX | 1991 |
| Delgado, David | USBP Del Rio, TX | 1998 |
| Delgado, Fernando | USBP Eagle Pass, TX | 1999 |
| Delgado, Joseph | Fire Marshal El Paso, TX | 1993 |
| Delgado, Sergio | USBP Eagle Pass, TX | 1997 |
| De Los Santos, Isaac | USBP Del Rio, TX | 1998 |
| Delrie, Maxie | USBP Rocksprings, TX | 1998 |
| Deluna, Fernando A. | USBP Laredo South, TX | 2000 |
| Deluna, Mario | USBP Cotulla, TX | 1999 |
| Deluna, Rudy, Jr. | USBP Laredo, TX | 1999 |
| Demine, Thomas E. | USBP Carrizo Springs, TX | 1997 |
| Deneweth, Anthony | USBP Willcox, AZ | 2002 |
| Densmore, Matthew J. | USBP Naco, AZ | 2002 |

| | | |
|---|---|---|
| Detrolio, Frank T. | Grant County S/O, WA | 1993 |
| Diaz, Armando | USBP Cotulla, TX | 1999 |
| Diaz, Hector | USBP Eagle Pass, TX | 1997 |
| Diaz, Jose | USBP Eagle Pass, TX | 2001 |
| Dill, Charles Jr. | USBP Harlingen, TX | 1993 |
| Dillender, William W. | USBP Detroit, MI | 1994 |
| Dirks, Nic | Grant County S/O, WA | 1993 |
| Dissler, John R. | USBP Comstock, TX | 2001 |
| Domenech, Erick R. | USBP Brackettville, TX | 2000 |
| Dominguez, James R. | USBP Uvalde, TX | 2001 |
| Donaghy, Shannon | USBP Del Rio, TX | 1998 |
| Donnelly, Sean E. | USBP Eagle Pass, TX | 2000 |
| Doran, James | USBP Laredo North, TX | 2000 |
| Doucet, Nicholas L. | US Customs-Air, San Angelo, TX | 1998 |
| Douglas, Mark S. | USBP Carrizo Springs, TX | 1999/00 |
| Dowdy, William | Springfield P.D., MO | 1993 |
| Downey, Joseph | Grant County S/O, Ephrata, WA | 1999 |
| Downs, Cory | US/INS San Antonio, TX | 2003 |
| Doyle, James W. | USBP Del Rio, TX | 1997 |
| Drollinger, William | Spokane P.D., WA | 1993 |
| Drummond, Dan | Renewable Resources, Yukon | 1994 |
| Dubbe, Erik P. | USBP Fresno, CA | 1991 |
| Duberstein, Kevin | US/INS Austin, TX | 2003 |
| Duff, Craig | USBP Del Rio, TX | 2000 |
| Duncan, Jeffrey | USBP Brackettville, TX | 1997 |
| Duncan, Lonnie | USBP Trenton, MI | 1994 |
| Dunn, David A. | USBP Spokane, WA | 2001 |
| Durham, Thomas K. | US Probation Pecos, TX | 1993 |
| Dushane, Greg P. | USBP Grand Rapids, MI | 1994 |
| Dusterhoff, Wayne C. | Glacier County S/O, MT | 1998 |
| Dye, Larry J. | USBP Wenatchee, WA | 2001 |
| Earl, Edwin | USBP Detroit, MI | 1994 |
| Easley, Roger L. | USBP Del Rio, TX | 1997 |
| Easterling, Lloyd M. | USBP Eagle Pass, TX | 2001 |
| Easton, Brent L. | INS Seattle, WA | 1991 |
| Edelberg, Michael M. | Sanders County S/O, MT | 1996 |

| | | |
|---|---|---|
| Edgard, Patrick M. | USBP Brackettville, TX | 1998 |
| Edie, Darwin K. | Grant County S/O, WA | 1993 |
| Edmiston, Justin O. | USBP Eagle Pass, TX | 1997/00 |
| Edwards, Catherine B. | USBP Laredo South, TX | 2000 |
| Edwards, John D. | USBP Carrizo Springs, TX | 1997 |
| Edwards, Jonathan F. | USBP Carrizo Springs, TX | 1997 |
| Ehresman, Roy W. | USBP Uvalde, TX | 2001 |
| Eichel, Patricia S. | INS Seattle, WA | 1993 |
| Elizade, Oscar L. | USBP Alamogordo, NM | 1991 |
| Elizondo, Bernardo | USBP Brackettville, TX | 1998 |
| Enriquez, Ruben | USBP Eagle Pass, TX | 1997/00 |
| Ensz, Thomas | USBP Fort Hancock, TX | 1997 |
| Erickson, Jeffery | Montana State Prison, MT | 1997/98 |
| Erickson, Mike | Glasgow P.D., MT | 1998 |
| Erskine, Thomas R. | USBP Roseburg, OR | 1994 |
| Erni, Paul K. | USBP Spokane, WA | 2001 |
| Ervin, William | USBP Spokane, WA | 2001 |
| Escamilla, Leticia | USBP Del Rio, TX | 1998 |
| Escamilla, Ricardo J. | USBP Laredo, TX | 1999 |
| Escamilla, Richardo | USBP Eagle Pass, TX | 1997 |
| Escontrias, Silverio | USBP Laredo, TX | 1999 |
| Esparza, Dionel F. | USBP Eagle Pass, TX | 1997 |
| Esparza, Mario F. | USBP Eagle Pass, TX | 1997 |
| Espinoza, Raul | USBP Eagle Pass, TX | 2000 |
| Esquivel, Javier | USBP Del Rio, TX | 1998 |
| Essing, Darryl | USBP Bellingham, WA | 1994 |
| Evans, William C. | Colville Tribal Police, WA | 1993 |
| Even, David J. | USBP Eagle Pass, TX | 1992/97 |
| Ewbank, David | Bothell, WA | 1996 |
| Fakmreddin, Mohammed | USBP Spokane, WA | 2001 |
| Falcon, Guadalupe | USBP Comstock, TX | 2001 |
| Farline, Larry W. | USBP Blaine, WA | 1994 |
| Fasig, Jack | Montana Dept. Corrections, MT | 1997 |
| Fay, Patrick | USBP Eagle Pass, TX | 1999 |
| Fehlman, Shawn | USBP Eagle Pass, TX | 2001 |
| Ferguson, Bill T. | USBP Uvalde, TX | 1998 |

| | | |
|---|---|---|
| Ferguson, Joe Don | USBP Brackettville, TX | 1998 |
| Figueroa, Nancy | USBP Laredo North, TX | 2000 |
| Finney, John W. III | USBP San Angelo, TX | 1998 |
| Fischer, Fred | Montana State Prison, MT | 1998 |
| Fisher, Carl A. | USBP Carrizo Springs, TX | 2001 |
| Fisher, Kenneth R. | USBP Carrizo Springs, TX | 2001 |
| Fisher, Nicholas C. | USBP Port Huron, MI | 1994 |
| Fisher Richard | USBP Laredo North, TX | 2000 |
| Fisher, Timothy (Mike) | USBP Whitefish, MT | 1993/01 |
| Fleenor, Grady L. | USBP Eureka, MT | 2001 |
| Fletcher, Sam R. | Burlington Northern R.R. | 1993 |
| Flores, Juan Jose | USBP Eagle Pass, TX | 1997/00 |
| Flores, Miguel A. | USBP Del Rio, TX | 1997 |
| Flores, Steven J. | USBP Brackettville, TX | 1998 |
| Fox, Curtis E. | USBP Del Rio, TX | 2000 |
| Fox, William T. | USBP Eagle Pass, TX | 1999 |
| Frankish, Ken | Renewable Resources, Yukon | 1994 |
| Frausto, Robert | US/INS Laredo, TX | 2003 |
| Freeman, Patrick | USBP Freer, TX | 1999 |
| Fuentes, Richard, Jr. | USBP Laredo North, TX | 2000 |
| Fuentes, Robert D. | USBP Eagle Pass, TX | 1997 |
| Fuestez, Oscar | USBP Brackettville, TX | 1998 |
| Fuller, Michael | USBP Carrizo Springs, TX | 2000 |
| Gallo, George | USBP Uvalde, TX | 1998 |
| Garcia. Alfredo | USBP San Angelo, TX | 1998 |
| Garcia, Carlos | USBP San Angelo, TX | 1992 |
| Garcia, Felix | USBP Brackettville, TX | 2000 |
| Garcia, James E. | USBP Eagle Pass, TX | 1997 |
| Garcia, Joe A. | USBP Laredo North, TX | 2000 |
| Garcia, Jose A. | USBP Eagle Pass, TX | 1997 |
| Garcia, Refugio, Jr. | USBP Del Rio, TX | 2000 |
| Garcia, Rene' | USBP Uvalde, TX | 1998 |
| Garcia, Roberto | USBP Eagle Pass, TX | 1997/00 |
| Garcia, Ronald D. | USBP Laredo South, TX | 2000 |
| Garcia, Rudy G. | USBP Del Rio, TX | 2000 |
| Garcia, Victor | USBP Laredo, TX | 1999 |

| | | |
|---|---|---|
| Garibay, Antonio III | USBP San Angelo, TX | 1998 |
| Garrett, Steven | USBP Fresno, CA | 1991 |
| Garrison, Art | Montana State Prison, MT | 1997 |
| Garrison, Brent C. | Burlington Northern R.R. | 1993 |
| Garza, Amancio III | USBP Carrizo Springs, TX | 1997 |
| Garza, Braulio, Jr. | USBP Eagle Pass, TX | 1997 |
| Garza, Hervey | USBP Comstock, TX | 2000 |
| Garza, Manuel, Jr. | USBP Carrizo Springs, TX | 2000 |
| Garza, Mario | USBP Detroit, MI | 1994 |
| Garza, Oscar B. | US/INS San Antonio, TX | 2003 |
| Gaytan, Miguel | USBP Comstock, TX | 1998 |
| Geach, Robert | Montana State Prison, MT | 1997/98 |
| Gearhart, Ron | Ravall County S/O, MT | 1997 |
| Gendreau, Errwyn | Montana State Prison, MT | 1998 |
| George, A. Morris | Renewable Resources, Yukon | 1995 |
| George, Edward J. | US Customs-Air San Angelo, TX | 1993 |
| Gerth, Dan | USBP Oroville, WA | 1993/01 |
| Gervol, Brian | USBP Blaine, WA | 1994 |
| Gillenwater, James M. | US Customs-Air San Angelo, TX | 1993 |
| Gillespie, Maynard L. | Spokane P.D., WA | 1993 |
| Gillies, Jerry W. | USBP Whitefish, MT | 1993/01 |
| Gillis, Gregg | RCMP Delta, B.C. | 1996 |
| Gilmore, Robert J. | USBP Laredo, TX | 2000 |
| Gleckman, Daniel | USBP Eagle Pass, TX | 1999 |
| Glycenfer, William A. | Burlington Northern R.R. | 1993 |
| Gomez, Alberico M. | USBP Laredo South, TX | 2000 |
| Gomez, Juan | USBP Uvalde, TX | 2000 |
| Gomez, Rafael (Ralph) | USBP Del Rio, TX | 1997 |
| Gonterman, Lee | Burlington Northern R.R. | 1993 |
| Gonzales, A.D., Jr. | USBP Eagle Pass, TX | 1997 |
| Gonzales, Adan D. | USBP Carrizo Springs, TX | 2000 |
| Gonzales, James P. | USBP Cotulla, TX | 1999 |
| Gonzales, Pete C. | US/INS San Antonio, TX | 2003 |
| Gonzales, Robert, Jr. | USBP Carrizo Springs, TX | 1997 |
| Gonzales, Rodolfo R. | US/INS San Antonio, TX | 2003 |
| Gonzalez, Carlos | USBP Uvalde, TX | 1998 |

| | | |
|---|---|---|
| Gonsaléz, David I. | USBP Laredo South, TX | 2000 |
| Gonzalez, Gerarado, | USBP Del Rio, TX | 1997 |
| Gonzalez, Giovanni | USBP Eagle Pass, TX | 2000/01 |
| Gonzalez, Gustavo | USBP Eagle Pass, TX | 2001 |
| Gonzalez, Mark | US/INS San Antonio, TX | 2003 |
| Gonzalez, Norman | USBP Eagle Pass, TX | 1999 |
| Gonzalez, Raymond E. | USBP Brackettville, TX | 2000 |
| Gonzales, Robert, Jr. | USBP Zapata, TX | 1999 |
| Gonzalez, Roel G. | US/INS Laredo, TX | 2003 |
| Gonzalez, Rolando T. | USBP Carrizo Springs, TX | 2000 |
| Gonzalez, Sergio | USBP Del Rio, TX | 1998 |
| Goodmanson, Douglas | USBP Del Rio, TX | 2000 |
| Gould, Edwin | USBP Laredo South, TX | 2000 |
| Gove, Gary C. | INS Spokane, WA | 1991 |
| Graham, Richard M., Jr. | USBP Oroville, WA | 2001 |
| Graham, Sherry | USBP Del Rio, TX | 1998 |
| Grant, Finley J. | Moses Lake, WA | 1994 |
| Grant, Scott | USBP Del Rio, TX | 2000 |
| Graves, Andre B. | USBP Eagle Pass, TX | 1997 |
| Green, Bryan | USBP Oroville, WA | 2001 |
| Green, James K. | USBP Eagle Pass, TX | 1997 |
| Gregg, James B. | Moses Lake, WA | 1993 |
| Gregg, Tim | Seattle, WA | 1996 |
| Grimm, Gerald | FLETC Artesia, NM | 1998 |
| Grout, Charles R. | USBP Cotulla, TX | 1993 |
| Guaderrama, Gilbert V. | USBP Sierra Blanca, TX | 1991 |
| Guajardo, Alberto | USBP Eagle Pass, TX | 1997 |
| Guajardo, David, Jr. | USBP Livermore, CA | 1991 |
| Guerra, Ignacia, III | USBP Carrizo Springs, TX | 1997 |
| Guerrero, Ludim | US/INS Laredo, TX | 2003 |
| Guerrero, Ricardo | USBP Carrizo Springs, TX | 2000 |
| Guidry, Earl P. | Lafayette Parish S/O, LA | 1992 |
| Guillen, Omar | USBP Laredo, TX | 1999 |
| Gustafson, Kris | Renewable Resources, Yukon | 1994 |
| Gutierrez, Francisco | USBP Laredo North, TX | 2000 |
| Gutierrez, Miguel | USBP Eagle Pass, TX | 1997/00 |

| | | |
|---|---|---|
| Guzman, Antonio | USBP Carrizo Springs, TX | 1997 |
| Guzman, David R. | USBP Hebbronville, TX | 1999 |
| Guzman, Luis | USBP San Antonio, TX | 1999 |
| Habib, Michael J. | USBP Lynden, WA | 1994 |
| Haines, Randy S. | USBP Naco, AZ | 2002 |
| Hale, Christopher | USBP Del Rio, TX | 2000 |
| Hall, Mark P. | USBP Detroit, MI | 1994 |
| Hall, Richard E. | US Customs-Air San Angelo, TX | 1993 |
| Halydier, James R. | FLETC Artesia, NM | 1998 |
| Hamrick, Richard L. | US/INS San Antonio, TX | 2003 |
| Handy, Robert | USBP Spokane, WA | 1993 |
| Hannie, Nicol E. | Lafayette Parish S/O, LA | 1991 |
| Hanson, Michael W. | USBP Eagle Pass, TX | 1999 |
| Hanson, Stanley | USBP Eagle Pass, TX | 1997/00 |
| Hardin, Cody R. | USBP Comstock, TX | 2001 |
| Harding, Thomas | INS Seattle, WA | 1991 |
| Hardt, Robert W. | USBP Eagle Pass, TX | 1997/00 |
| Hardt, Wm. (Mongo) | USBP Laredo, TX | 1999 |
| Harlan, Martin P. | USBP Comstock, TX | 1998 |
| Harmon, Carl L. | USBP Ysleta, TX | 1991 |
| Harris, Glenn S. | USBP Carrizo Springs, TX | 2001 |
| Harris, Gordon E. | Grant County S/O, WA | 1993 |
| Harris, Jonathan | USBP Carrizo Springs, TX | 2000 |
| Harris, Steve | Walla Walla P.D., WA | 1996 |
| Harris, Vines E. | US/INS San Antonio, TX | 2003 |
| Harsa, Barry, Jr. | USBP Laredo South, TX | 2000 |
| Harshbarger, Vincent | USBP Bowbells, ND | 1994 |
| Hart, Walter T. | US Customs-Air San Angelo, TX | 1993 |
| Harvey, Larence E. | USBP Oxnard, CA | 1991 |
| Hatcher, Douglas | USBP Carrizo Springs, TX | 2000 |
| Hatfield, Jim R. | Fed.Law Enforcement Training Ctr, GA | 1996 |
| Hathaway, Harry H. | USBP Cotulla, TX | 1993 |
| Hatton, David M. | USBP Lynden, WA | 1994 |
| Hawkins, Fred A. | INS Seattle, WA | 1991 |
| Hay, Timothy | USBP Eagle Pass, TX | 2000 |
| Haynes, Clayton G. | USBP San Angelo, TX | 1998 |

| | | |
|---|---|---|
| Hazelton, Joseph L. | USBP Carrizo Springs, TX | 2000 |
| Hearne, Robert | USBP Eagle Pass, TX | 2000 |
| Heath, Christian L. | USBP Eagle Pass, TX | 1997 |
| Helbig, Larence, Jr. | USBP Uvalde, TX | 1998 |
| Helt, Robert W. III | USBP Uvalde, TX | 2001 |
| Helt, Shaun | USBP Laredo, TX | 1999 |
| Hernandez, Alexander | USBP Cotulla, TX | 1992 |
| Hernandez, Arturo | USBP Comstock, TX | 1998 |
| Hernandez, David J. | USBP Brackettville, TX | 2001 |
| Hernandez, Francisco | USBP Comstock, TX | 2000 |
| Hernandez, Javier | USBP Laredo South, TX | 2000 |
| Hernandez, Juan F. | US/INS San Antonio, TX | 2003 |
| Hernandez, Ruben | US/INS San Antonio, TX | 2003 |
| Hetu, John D. | USBP Brackettville, TX | 1998 |
| Hickman, Chad | USBP Del Rio, TX | 2001 |
| Higginbotham, Lewis | US Army-Retired, MT | 1993 |
| Hildick, Michael | USBP Uvalde, TX | 1998 |
| Hill, Carl L. | USBP Colville, WA | 1993 |
| Hill, Robert C. | INS Spokane, WA | 1991 |
| Hill, Sandy C. | USBP Comstock, TX | 1998 |
| Hiltz, Shawn | USBP Carrizo Springs, TX | 2000 |
| Hinojosa, Howard J. | USBP Del Rio, TX | 1998 |
| Hinojosa, Michael S. | US/INS San Antonio, TX | 2003 |
| Hise, Loyd K., Jr. | USBP Bakersfield, CA | 1991 |
| Hodges, Donald J. | USBP Las Cruces, NM | 1991 |
| Holguin, Donald P. | USBP Pasco, WA | 1993/01 |
| Holloway, Mark R. | USBP Detroit, MI | 1994 |
| Holman, Gerald L. | Grant County S/O, WA | 1993 |
| Holmes, Jonathan M. | USBP Alamogordo, NM | 1991 |
| Holmes, Randy | USBP Uvalde, TX | 1998 |
| Hopkins, Dave A. | Burlington Northern R.R. | 1993 |
| Horne, Vaughn G. | USBP Carrizo Springs, TX | 2000 |
| Hornik, Bruce W. | USBP Eagle Pass, TX | 2000 |
| Horton, Curtis | RCMP Whitehorse, Yukon | 1994 |
| Housler, Thomas P. | USBP Ysleta, TX | 1992 |
| Howarth, John | USBP San Angelo, TX | 1998 |

| | | |
|---|---|---|
| Hubbard, Michael | USBP Brackettville, TX | 1998 |
| Huber, Patrick H. | Montana State Prison, MT | 1997 |
| Hubert, John M. | USBP El Paso, TX | 1991 |
| Hudson, Darryl L. | Grant County S/O, Ephrata, WA | 2002 |
| Huizar, Joe L. | USBP Del Rio, TX | 2000 |
| Hunt, Terry | USBP Rocksprings, TX | 1998 |
| Hurney Thomas C. | USBP Del Rio, TX | 2000 |
| Hurst, Bradley Q. | USBP Eagle Pass, TX | 2000 |
| Hurst, Eldon W. | USBP Bonners Ferry, ID | 1993/01 |
| Hurst, Michael W. | USBP Richland, WA | 2001 |
| Hyer, Collin | Grant County S/O, Ephrata, WA | 2002 |
| Ibarra, Joe A. | US/INS San Antonio, TX | 2003 |
| Irizarry, Edgar R. | USBP Eagle Pass, TX | 1999 |
| Izquierdo, David | USBP Brackettville, TX | 2000 |
| Jackson, Claude A. | USBP Twin Falls, ID | 1994 |
| Jackson, Jimmy D. | USBP Uvalde, TX | 1997 |
| Jackson, Thomas, Jr. | Burlington Northern R.R. | 1997 |
| James, Barry P. | USBP Laredo South, TX | 2000 |
| Jauhola, Ron | USBP Duluth, MN | 1994 |
| Jauregui, Julio | USBP Eagle Pass, TX | 1999 |
| Jensen, William C. | US/INS San Antonio, TX | 2003 |
| Jerde, Steve | USBP Bottineau, ND | 1994 |
| Jimenez, Frank | USBP Port Isabel, TX | 1993 |
| Jimenez, Joe A. | USBP Carrizo Springs, TX | 2001 |
| Joachim, Richard M. | FLETC Artesia, NM | 1998 |
| Johnson, Charles, Jr. | USBP Blaine, WA | 1994 |
| Johnson, Gregory | USBP Uvalde, TX | 1997 |
| Johnson, Jerry | USBP Del Rio, TX | 1997 |
| Johnson, Michael D. | USBP Del Rio, TX | 1994/98 |
| Johnson, Roy C. | USBP Eureka, MT | 1993 |
| Johnson, Steven P. | Moses Lake P.D., WA | 1991 |
| Johnston, James L. | USBP Roseburg, OR | 1994 |
| Johnston, Randall | USBP San Antonio, TX | 1999 |
| Johnston, Royce R. | USBP Portal, ND | 1994 |
| Jolles, Jeremy S. | USBP Del Rio, TX | 2000 |
| Jones, Cavin | US Customs-Air San Angelo, TX | 1998 |

| | | |
|---|---|---|
| Jones, Clyde L. | USBP San Angelo, TX | 1998 |
| Jones, Jamie D. | US/INS San Antonio, TX | 2003 |
| Jones, Jeff C. | USBP Del Rio, TX | 1997 |
| Jones, Jerry W. | US Customs-Air San Angelo, TX | 1993/98 |
| Jones, Martin A. | US Customs-Air San Angelo, TX | 1992 |
| Jovanovich, Joseph S. | USBP Blaine, WA | 1994 |
| Juarez, Omar | US/INS Laredo, TX | 2003 |
| Judice, Kip A. | Lafayette Parish S/O, LA | 1992 |
| Justice, Lehman G. | USBP El Paso, TX | 1991 |
| Justus, David K. | USBP Eagle Pass, TX | 1997/00 |
| Karhoff, Russell A. | USBP Scobey, MT | 1994 |
| Kartchner, Steven T. | USBP Douglas, AZ | 2002 |
| Keene, Kenneth M. | USBP Comstock, TX | 1998 |
| Keller, David M. | USBP Lynden, WA | 1994 |
| Kemmett, Bryan W. | USBP Carrizo Springs, TX | 1997 |
| Kent, Marty | Bozeman P.D., MT | 1996 |
| Kersey, Jeremy | USBP Carrizo Springs, TX | 2000 |
| Ketzler, John C. | USBP San Angelo, TX | 1998 |
| Kieffer, Anthony L. | USBP San Angelo, TX | 1998 |
| Kilpatrick, Robert C. | USBP Comstock, TX | 2000 |
| Kimbro, John | USBP Comstock, TX | 2000 |
| King, Frank R. | USBP Uvalde, TX | 1998 |
| King, J. Thomas | USBP Grand Rapids, MI | 1994 |
| Kingery, Raymond | USBP Laredo, TX | 1993 |
| Kingery, Raymond (Glen) | US/INS Eden, TX | 2003 |
| Kjeldgaard, Lisette | USBP Brackettville, TX | 2000 |
| Kluge, Gerald A | USBP Laredo North, TX | 2000 |
| Knain, Scott A. | USBP Grand Forks, ND | 1994 |
| Kneeskern, Paul | USBP Comstock, TX | 1998 |
| Knoll, Mark S. | USBP Brackettville, TX | 2000 |
| Knutson, Greg J. | Grant County S/O, Ephrata, WA | 2002 |
| Knutson, Ken | Renewable Resources, Yukon | 1995 |
| Kohlman, Jonathan M. | USBP Blaine, WA | 1994 |
| Kohlman, Robert | USBP Lynden, WA | 1994 |
| Konkle, Daniel T. | USBP Comstock, TX | 2000 |
| Kowalski, Stephen K. | USBP Eagle Pass, TX | 1999 |

| | | |
|---|---|---|
| Kracher, Jerry L. | USBP Fresno, CA | 1991 |
| Kraemer, P. Sean | USBP Carrizo Springs, TX | 2000 |
| Krause, Stan | USBP Eureka, MT | 2001 |
| Kreowski, Kevin C. | USBP Spokane, WA | 1993 |
| Kriete, Joe | Grant County S/O, Ephrata, WA | 2002 |
| Kuecker, Gerald E. | US Customs-Air San Angelo, TX | 1993 |
| Kuperstein, Alan T. | USBP Eagle Pass, TX | 2000 |
| Lacey, Brian Patrick | Renewable Resources, Yukon | 1995 |
| Lackey, Craig R. | USBP Laredo North, TX | 2000 |
| Lacombe, Andrew J. | USBP Del Rio, TX | 1993 |
| Lake, Gordon K. | USBP El Paso, TX | 1991 |
| LaMascus, David | USBP Uvalde, TX | 1998 |
| LaMascus, Steven | USBP Del Rio, TX | 1998 |
| Lambert, Arlington | USBP Eagle Pass, TX | 1999 |
| Lambowne, Timothy W. | USBP Brownsville, TX | 1993 |
| Lamont, Raymond, Jr. | USBP Laredo South, TX | 2000 |
| Lane, David L. | US/INS Austin, TX | 2003 |
| Langford, Alan L. | USBP Sweetgrass, MT | 1994 |
| LaPage, Sheppard | USBP Carrizo Springs, TX | 2000 |
| LaQuey, William J. | USBP Sonoita, AZ | 2002 |
| Laracuente, Habacuc | USBP Del Rio, TX | 1997 |
| Laredo, Emmanuel | USBP Uvalde, TX | 2000 |
| Lario, Glenn R. | Fisheries & Oceans, Yukon | 1994 |
| Laroque, Lorne | Renewable Resources, Yukon | 1995 |
| Lausell, Gilberto | USBP Laredo, TX | 2000 |
| Lawson, Charles D. | USBP Uvalde, TX | 2001 |
| Lawyer, David K. | USBP Del Rio, TX | 1997 |
| Leal, Hilario, Jr. | USBP Del Rio, TX | 1997 |
| Leal, James | USBP Comstock, TX | 1998 |
| Leal, Rodolfo | USBP Zapata, TX | 1999 |
| Leal Donald J. | USBP Del Rio, TX | 1998 |
| Lehner, Robert L. | Montana State Prison, MT | 1998 |
| Leigh, Larry | Renewable Resources, Yukon | 1995 |
| Leigh, Trey | USBP Del Rio, TX | 2000 |
| Leigh, Wm (Trey), III | USBP Carrizo Springs, TX | 1997 |
| Lennon, Troy | USBP Comstock, TX | 2000 |

| | | |
|---|---|---|
| Letsinger, Gary C. | USBP Brackettville, TX | 1998 |
| Lewis, Stephen | USBP Eagle Pass, TX | 1997 |
| Licking, Matthew M. | El Paso County S/O, TX | 1993 |
| Lieurance, Matthew O. | USBP San Angelo, TX | 1992 |
| Lindemann, Robert E. | USBP Detroit, MI | 1994 |
| Lira, Hector D. | USBP Laredo North, TX | 2000 |
| Loftin, Billy R. | USBP Del Rio, TX | 1997 |
| Longorid, Johnny E. | USBP Carrizo Springs, TX | 2001 |
| Loomis, Harold, Jr. | USBP Lordsburg, NM | 2003 |
| Lopez, Alexis | USBP Comstock, TX | 1997 |
| Lopez, Carlos A. | USBP Eagle Pass, TX | 1997 |
| Lopez, Eduardo J. | USBP Del Rio, TX | 2000 |
| Lopez, Francisco, Jr. | USBP Del Rio, TX | 1998 |
| Lopez, Juan | USBP Del Rio, TX | 2000 |
| Lopez-Mossman, Loretta | USBP El Paso, TX | 1991/01 |
| Lopez, Marco A. | USBP Casa Grande, AZ | 2002 |
| Lopez-Perez, Roberrto | USBP Laredo North, TX | 2000 |
| Lovett, Shane | USBP Carrizo Springs, TX | 2000 |
| Lozano, Cesar | USBP Del Rio, TX | 1998 |
| Lucas, William B. | US/INS Eden, TX | 2003 |
| Luedecke, John | USBP Eagle Pass, TX | 2000 |
| Luisi, Tony | San Jose Pd, San Jose, CA | 2001 |
| Luna, Ruben H. | USBP Comstock, TX | 2000 |
| Luna, Sandra | USBP Laredo, TX | 2000 |
| Lundgren, Kent E. | INS Yakima, WA | 1991 |
| Lyons, Lace R. | USBP Del Rio, TX | 2000 |
| Machidon, Cristian | INS Seattle, WA | 1993 |
| MacKay, Timothy N. | USBP Malta, MT | 1994 |
| MacLeod, Rod A. | RCMP N. Vancouver, Canada | 1996 |
| Madrid, Bernardo R. | USBP Bakersfield, CA | 1991 |
| Madrid, Presley E. | USBP Laredo North, TX | 2000 |
| Madrid, Ruben J. | USBP Eagle Pass, TX | 1997 |
| Mahtesian, Matthew | USBP Uvalde, TX | 1998 |
| Malcomb, Thomas C. | Montana State Prison, MT | 1998 |
| Malone, John W. Jr. | USBP Ajo, AZ | 2002 |
| Manning, Hal | USBP Uvalde, TX | 1998 |

| | | |
|---|---|---|
| Marcelino, Alegria | USBP Eagle Pass, TX | 2001 |
| Marcos, Charles | USBP Laredo North, TX | 2000 |
| Maresh, Michael L. | USBP Del Rio, TX | 1997 |
| Markle, Herbert H. | USBP Sault St Marie, MI | 1994 |
| Marley, Neil Harris | USBP Eagle Pass, TX | 1997 |
| Marmolejo, Vincent | USBP Carrizo Springs, TX | 2001 |
| Marquez, Mark D. | USBP Bakersfield, CA | 1991 |
| Marquez, Pablo | USBP Laredo South, TX | 2000 |
| Marsh, Les R. | USBP Laredo North, TX | 2000 |
| Marshall, Carl E. | USBP Eagle Pass, TX | 2000 |
| Marshall, Peter F. | USBP San Angelo, TX | 1993 |
| Martin, Jeremy | USBP Eagle Pass, TX | 1999/01 |
| Martinez, Adrian L. | USBP Del Rio, TX | 2000 |
| Martinez, Arthur R. | USBP Eagle Pass, TX | 1999 |
| Martinez, Gerald M. | USBP Comstock, TX | 1997 |
| Martinez, Jim | USBP Laredo, TX | 1999 |
| Martinez, Jorge B. | USBP Laredo South, TX | 2000 |
| Martinez, Jose C. | USBP Uvalde, TX | 2001 |
| Martinez, Jose R. | USBP Alamogordo, NM | 1991 |
| Martinez, Juan F. | USBP Uvalde, TX | 2001 |
| Martinez, Juan M. | US/INS San Antonio, TX | 2003 |
| Martinez, Monserrate | USBP El Paso, TX | 1993 |
| Martinez, Pete, III | US/INS Laredo, TX | 2003 |
| Martinez, Robert | USBP Eagle Pass, TX | 2000 |
| Martinez, Roy T. | USBP Laredo North, TX | 2000 |
| Marullo, Art A. | Lafayette Parish S/O, LA | 1992 |
| Massingill, Ronald | USBP Eagle Pass, TX | 1997 |
| Masters, Kenneth W. | USBP Laredo North, TX | 2000 |
| Mata, Luis O. | USBP Uvalde, TX | 1998 |
| Matney, David A. | Grant County S/O, Ephrata, WA | 1999 |
| May, Donald M. | Montana State Prison, MT | 1997 |
| Mayer, Gregory E. | USBP Eagle Pass, TX | 1999/00 |
| Mayer, William | USBP Del Rio, TX | 2000 |
| McBride, John P. | USBP Brackettville, TX | 1998 |
| McBroom, Chad E. | USBP Eagle Pass, TX | 1999 |
| McCarson, Mike | USBP Comstock, TX | 1998 |

| | | |
|---|---|---|
| McCauley, Scott E. | USBP Laredo North, TX | 2000 |
| McClymonds, Rocky | USBP Twin Falls, ID | 1994 |
| McCutchen, David | USBP Uvalde, TX | 1998 |
| McDowell, Terry | USBP Laredo North, TX | 2000 |
| McElligott, Tim | US/INS San Antonio, TX | 2003 |
| McElvene, Daryl | USBP Comstock, TX | 2001 |
| McEwen, Dustin | USBP Del Rio, TX | 2000 |
| McGillis, Nathan D. | USBP Del Rio, TX | 2000 |
| McGrath, Christopher | USBP Carrizo Springs, TX | 2000/01 |
| McGuigan, Chris A. | Sanders County S/O, MT | 1997 |
| McGuire, Cruz C. | USBP Del Rio, TX | 2000 |
| McGuire, Richard | USBP Brackettville, TX | 2001 |
| McKeever, Shawn M. | USBP Eagle Pass, TX | 1999 |
| McKinlay, Ronald | USBP Twin Falls, ID | 1994 |
| McKinney, Sean | USBP Del Rio, TX | 1997 |
| McLeod, Gary B. | RCMP Whitehorse, Yukon | 1994 |
| McLeroy, Jarod C. | USBP Carrizo Springs, TX | 2001 |
| McMillan, Cliffton | USBP Eagle Pass, TX | 2000 |
| McNeil, Scott | Montana State Prison, MT | 1998 |
| McPherson, Richard | USBP Abilene, TX | 1998 |
| McRorey, Kirby D. | Texas Parks & Wildlife, TX | 1992 |
| Meagher, Daniel S. | USBP Del Rio, TX | 2000 |
| Meagher, Mike | Montana State Prison, MT | 1998 |
| Meehleib, Scott | USBP Brackettville, TX | 2000 |
| Meek, Rick | USBP Laredo North, TX | 2000 |
| Mehlhoff, Daniel P. | USBP Blaine, WA | 1994 |
| Meister, Kirby A. | Renewable Resources, Yukon | 1994 |
| Meister, Roger | USBP Uvalde, TX | 1998 |
| Melott, Ted B. | FLETC Artesia, NM | 1998 |
| Mendoza, Javier | USBP Eagle Pass, TX | 1999 |
| Mendoza, Miguel | USBP Carrizo Springs, TX | 1997 |
| Mendoza, Noe | USBP Laredo North, TX | 2000 |
| Mendoza, Robert G. | Dimmit County S/O, TX | 1992 |
| Mendoza, William P. | USBP Eagle Pass, TX | 1997 |
| Meredith, Troy | USBP Carrizo Springs, TX | 1997 |
| Merkley, Nolen | Moses Lake, WA | 1994 |

| | | |
|---|---|---|
| Mestas, Ruben | USBP Brackettville, TX | 1998 |
| Metcalf, C.W. | US/INS San Antonio, TX | 2003 |
| Meza, John | USBP Del Rio, TX | 2000 |
| Michel, John H. III | USBP Wenatchee, WA | 2001 |
| Michelini, Dennis | USBP Carrizo Springs, TX | 1997 |
| Micu, Michael J. | Montana State Prison, MT | 1997 |
| Middleton, Mark | USBP Del Rio, TX | 2000 |
| Miera, Epifanio O. | FLETC Artesia, NM | 1998 |
| Miller, Aaron K. | USBP Bellingham, WA | 1994 |
| Miller, Bruce | Montana State Prison, MT | 1997 |
| Miller, Bryan L. | USBP El Paso, TX | 1991 |
| Miller, Freddy | US/INS San Antonio, TX | 2003 |
| Miller, John K. | USBP Carrizo Springs, TX | 2000 |
| Miller, Marty J. | Lafayette Parish S/O, LA | 1991 |
| Miller, Rickie D. | USBP Malta, MT | 1994 |
| Miller, Ronald D. | USBP Uvalde, TX | 1998 |
| Miller, Steve | MT. Dept. of Corrections, MT | 1997 |
| Miller, Terry R. | RCMP Whitehorse, Yukon | 1994 |
| Mills, Troy | USBP Lordsburg, NM | 2003 |
| Mingee, Robert | USBP Blaine, WA | 1994 |
| Mirabile, Carmen | USBP Del Rio, TX | 2000 |
| Mitchell, David | USBP Brackettville, TX | 2001 |
| Mitchell, William D. | USBP Trenton, MI | 1994 |
| Mizell, Matthew P. | USBP Carrizo Springs, TX | 1997 |
| Mobley, Jeremy C. | USBP Eagle Pass, TX | 2001 |
| Molaison, Raymond Jr. | USBP Eagle Pass, TX | 1997 |
| Molina, Alfredo | USBP Laredo South, TX | 2000 |
| Molinar, George | FLETC Artesia, NM | 1998 |
| Montemayor, Jose S. | US/INS San Antonio, TX | 2003 |
| Moody, David | USBP Brackettville, TX | 1998 |
| Moore, Donnie | USBP Brackettville, TX | 2000 |
| Moore, Harry V. | USBP Eagle Pass, TX | 1997/00 |
| Moore, Jason D. | USBP Del Rio, TX | 2000 |
| Moore, Joshua | Montana State Prison, MT | 1998 |
| Moore, Kevin | Ephrata, WA | 1994 |
| Moore, Mike | Montana Fish, Wildlife & Parks, MT | 1996 |

| | | |
|---|---|---|
| Moore, Russell | USBP Brackettville, TX | 1997 |
| Moore, Rusty | USBP Brackettville, TX | 1998 |
| Mora, Steven G. | USBP Brackettville, TX | 2000 |
| Mora, Steven G. | US/INS San Antonio, TX | 2003 |
| Morales, Pablo, Jr. | USBP Uvalde, TX | 1998 |
| Moran, Michael P. | USBP Sierra Blanca, TX | 1991 |
| Moreno, Miguel A. | USBP Del Rio, TX | 1998 |
| Morgan, Timothy | USBP Eagle Pass, TX | 1997 |
| Moring, Thomas L. | Lewistown P.D., MT | 1996 |
| Morrell, Art R. | USBP Eagle Pass, TX | 1999/00 |
| Moses, Robert | USBP Cotulla, TX | 1999 |
| Mossman, Bill | INS Spokane, WA | 2001 |
| Mouton, Todd M. | Lafayette Parish S/O, LA | 1992 |
| Moyer, Stephen E. | USBP Eagle Pass, TX | 1999 |
| Mullings, Brent A. | Grant County S/O, Ephrata, WA | 1999 |
| Munson, Brian | USBP Detroit, MI | 1994 |
| Munoz, Jesus, Jr. | USBP Eagle Pass, TX | 1997 |
| Munoz, Robert C. | USBP Eagle Pass, TX | 2001 |
| Murphy, Greg | USBP Carrizo Springs, TX | 1997 |
| Murphy, Matt | Montana Fish, Wildlife & Parks, MT | 1996 |
| Murphy, Robert A. | USBP Blaine, WA | 1994 |
| Murphy, William G. | USBP Carrizo Springs, TX | 1992 |
| Murray, Stephen M. | INS Yakima, WA | 1991 |
| Myers, Michael W. | USBP Brackettville, TX | 2001 |
| Myers, Stan | USBP Uvalde, TX | 2000 |
| Myhre, Kevin | Lewistown P.D., MT | 1996 |
| Nason, Bruce | USBP Uvalde, TX | 1998 |
| Navarro, Juan | USBP Laredo, TX | 2000 |
| Nelson, Kurt | USBP Scobey, MT | 1994 |
| Nemitz, Richard | USBP Trenton, MI | 1994 |
| Nevarez, Efrain, Jr. | USBP Uvalde, TX | 2000 |
| Newton, Robert P. | USBP Eagle Pass, TX | 1999 |
| Nice, Michael D. | USBP Del Rio, TX | 1997 |
| Nichols, Kevin | Montana Fish, Wildlife & Parks, MT | 1996 |
| Niles, Steve | US/INS San Antonio, TX | 2003 |
| Nilson, Dale H. | USBP Whitefish, MT | 1993/01 |

| | | |
|---|---|---|
| Noble, Dean L. | USBP Eagle Pass, TX | 1999 |
| Noriega, Rene C. | USBP Bakersfield, CA | 1991 |
| Not Afraid, Marlin | Crow Tribal Agency, MT | 1998 |
| Nowacki, Gary F. | USBP Grand Forks, ND | 1994 |
| Nunex, Mark A. | USBP Del Rio, TX | 1997 |
| Nunez, Hector | USBP Eagle Pass, TX | 1999 |
| Nussrallah, Robert J. | USBP Eagle Pass, TX | 1992 |
| Nutt, Steven | USBP Laredo South, TX | 2000 |
| O'Brien, John R. | USBP Port Huron, MI | 1994 |
| Oechsli, George W. | USBP Pecos, TX | 1993 |
| Oechsli, George | US/INS Eden, TX | 2003 |
| O'Leary, Marisol V. | USBP Eagle Pass, TX | 2001 |
| Olmos. David | USBP Del Rio, TX | 2000 |
| Oloff, Jerry H. | USBP Twin Falls, ID | 1994 |
| Olson, Brian F. | USBP Pembina, ND | 1994 |
| Olson, Gary | INS Seattle, WA | 1991 |
| Olson, Keith M. | USBP Bellingham, WA | 1994 |
| O'Malley, John P. | Grant County S/O, Ephrata, WA | 2002 |
| O'Neill, Dennis C. | USBP Del Rio, TX | 2000 |
| Ontiveros, Armando | Carrizo Springs, TX | 2000 |
| O'Reilly, Ian | USBP Laredo North, TX | 2000 |
| Ornelas, Ruben, Jr. | USBP Eagle Pass, TX | 1999 |
| Ortega, Harold | USBP Uvalde, TX | 2001 |
| Ortega, Sylvester M. | US/INS San Antonio, TX | 2003 |
| Ortiz, Diana | USBP Carrizo Springs, TX | 2000 |
| Ortiz, Roxana | USBP Comstock, TX | 2001 |
| Osborne, Brian | USBP Del Rio, TX | 2000 |
| Palomo, Humberto | US/INS San Antonio, TX | 2003 |
| Partida, Jesus M. | USBP Eagle Pass, TX | 2001 |
| Payne, Joshua B. | USBP Carrizo Springs, TX | 2001 |
| Pearse, Fred | USBP Tucson, AZ | 2002 |
| Pena, Jesus G. | USBP Tucson, AZ | 2002 |
| Perez, Larry | USBP Carrizo Springs, TX | 2001 |
| Pilkington, Jeffrey | USBP Brackettville, TX | 2001 |
| Pinkerton, Lealan L. | USBP Spokane, WA | 2001 |
| Porter, Charles M. | FLETC Artesia, NM | 1998 |

| | | |
|---|---|---|
| Postulka, Lon | USBP Bonners Ferry, ID | 2001 |
| Prejean, James | USBP Eagle Pass, TX | 1999 |
| Preto, Edward | RCMP Pelly Crossing, Yukon | 1994 |
| Pryor, Brett C. | Carencro P.D., LA | 1992 |
| Puente, David | USBP Brackettville, TX | 2001 |
| Puente, Omar | USBP Laredo, TX | 1999 |
| Putnam, John V. | USBP Spokane, WA | 1993 |
| Pyatte, David | USBP Comstock, TX | 1998 |
| Qualia, Mark L. | USBP Del Rio, TX | 2000 |
| Queen, Barry J. | USBP Eagle Pass, TX | 1999 |
| Quevedo, Carlos A. | USBP Carrizo Springs, TX | 1997 |
| Quczada, Manuel | USBP Eagle Pass, TX | 1997 |
| Quigg, Joseph G. | USBP El Paso, TX | 1993 |
| Quinones, Eugenio, Jr. | USBP Laredo South, TX | 2000 |
| Quinones, William E. | USBP Uvalde, TX | 1998 |
| Quintana, Juan | USBP Carrizo Springs, TX | 2000 |
| Ramirez, Alberto G. | USBP Laredo North, TX | 2000 |
| Ramirez, Dolores "Lolo" | USBP Comstock, TX | 1997/00/01 |
| Ramirez, Edvardo | USBP Uvalde, TX | 1998 |
| Ramirez, Mario | USBP Comstock, TX | 2000 |
| Ramirez, Michael | USBP Eagle Pass, TX | 1999 |
| Ramirez, Nabor E. | USBP Eagle Pass, TX | 1997 |
| Ramirez, Randy S. | USBP Del Rio, TX | 2000 |
| Ramon, Gerardo D. | USBP Del Rio, TX | 2000 |
| Ramos, Andres III | USBP Laredo, TX | 1999 |
| Ramos, Manuel S. | USBP Eagle Pass, TX | 1997 |
| Ramsey, Brian L. | USBP Laredo South, TX | 2000 |
| Ramus, Jesus R. | US/INS San Antonio, TX | 2003 |
| Rangel, Jaime | USBP Carrizo Springs, TX | 1992 |
| Rasmussen, Dane J.A. | USBP Laredo North, TX | 2000 |
| Rasmussen, Heather | USBP Carrizo Springs, TX | 2001 |
| Raven, Terry L. | US Customs-Air San Angelo, TX | 1993 |
| Reed, Gordon D. | USBP Warroad, MN | 1994 |
| Reed, Gregory P. | USBP Oroville, WA | 1993/01 |
| Reed, Jay W. | USBP Fowlerton, TX | 1992 |
| Reed, Michael J. | Montana Lea Helena, MT | 1996 |

| | | |
|---|---|---|
| Reeve, Robert D. | USBP Douglas, AZ | 2002 |
| Reif, Jordon L. | US Customs-Air San Angelo, TX | 1993 |
| Reilly, Michael J. | USBP Del Rio, TX | 1997 |
| Reinhardt, Randall | USBP Carrizo Springs, TX | 2000 |
| Renken, Ronald M. | Grant County S/O, WA | 1993 |
| Reno, Shane | Montana Fish, Wildlife & Parks, MT | 1998 |
| Reome, Wayne M. | USBP Spokane, WA | 1993 |
| Resma, Mario A. | USBP Carrizo Springs, TX | 2000 |
| Reusch, Christian L. | USBP Del Rio, TX | 2000 |
| Reyes, Fernando | USBP Brownsville, TX | 1993 |
| Reyes, Jaime | USBP Laredo North, TX | 2000 |
| Reyna, George A. | USBP Laredo North, TX | 2000 |
| Reyna, Ricardo | USBP Eagle Pass, TX | 1999 |
| Reynolds, Karey | Lake County S/O, MT | 1996 |
| Reza, Jorge L. | USBP Sierra Blanca, TX | 1991 |
| Rice, Ron | INS Seattle, WA | 1991 |
| Richard, Raymond | USBP Eagle Pass, TX | 1997 |
| Richards, Jonathan D. | USBP Ysleta, TX | 1991 |
| Rigsby, Randy E. | USBP San Angelo, TX | 1998 |
| Rimple, Steve | Moses Lake, WA | 1996 |
| Rios, Eleazar | USBP Brackettville, TX | 1998 |
| Rios, Mark A. | USBP Del Rio, TX | 2000 |
| Ritchey, Dan | Montana Fish, Wildlife & Parks, MT | 1997 |
| Ritchie, Robert E. | Washougal P.D., WA | 1996 |
| Rivera, Alejandro, Jr. | USBP Del Rio, TX | 1997 |
| Rivera, Ramon | USBP Del Rio, TX | 1998 |
| Robb, Leslie J. | US Customs-Air San Angelo, TX | 1992 |
| Roberts, James D. | FLETC Artesia, NM | 1998 |
| Roberts, Jim | Montana Fish, Wildlife & Parks, MT | 1997 |
| Robillard, Don | US/INS Austin, TX | 2003 |
| Robinson, Scott B. | USBP Warroad, MN | 1994 |
| Robles, David, Jr. | USBP Uvalde, TX | 1998 |
| Rocha, Alfredo, Jr. | USBP Carrizo Springs, TX | 2000 |
| Rocha, Arturo, Jr. | USBP Laredo, TX | 1999 |
| Rodriguez, Abraham | US/INS Eagle Pass, TX | 2003 |
| Rodriguez, Alex | USBP Eagle Pass, TX | 1997 |

| | | |
|---|---|---|
| Rodriguez, Andres A. | USBP Laredo North, TX | 2000 |
| Rodriguez, Ariel | USBP Carrizo Springs, TX | 2001 |
| Rodriguez, Blanca | USBP Eagle Pass, TX | 2000 |
| Rodriguez, Elisen | USBP Brackettville, TX | 1997 |
| Rodriguez, Enrique Jr. | USBP Eagle Pass, TX | 2001 |
| Rodriguez, Eugenio | USBP Laredo North, TX | 2000 |
| Rodriguez, Johnny J. | USBP Carrizo Springs, TX | 1997 |
| Rodriguez, Leonardo | USBP Brackettville, TX | 2000 |
| Rodriguez, Lonnie | USBP Del Rio, TX | 2000 |
| Rodriguez, Manuel, Jr. | USBP Eagle Pass, TX | 1999 |
| Rodriguez, Ramiro | USBP Carrizo Springs, TX | 1997 |
| Rodriguez, Rodolfo | USBP Eagle Pass, TX | 1997/00 |
| Rodzoch, Al J. | USBP Carrizo Springs, TX | 2000 |
| Roe, Dana D. | Hill County S/O, MT | 1998 |
| Roe, Rob, | Montana State Prison, MT | 1997 |
| Roel, Robert | USBP Oroville, WA | 2001 |
| Roger, Allan D. | Lafayette Parish S/O, LA | 1992 |
| Rogers, Andrew | USBP Comstock, TX | 2000 |
| Rogers, Andrew J. | USBP Eagle Pass, TX | 1992 |
| Rogers, Marc N. | USBP Uvalde, TX | 2001 |
| Rohde, Kenneth W. | USBP Eagle Pass, TX | 1999 |
| Rojas, Richard | USBP Eagle Pass, TX | 1999 |
| Romple, Christian | Yakima, WA | 2004 |
| Ronspiez, John P. | USBP San Angelo, TX | 1998 |
| Rook, Guy D. | RCMP Whitehorse, Yukon | 1995 |
| Rosales, Romulo, Jr. | USBP Eagle Pass, TX | 1999 |
| Rosas, Sandra A. | USBP Carrizo Springs, TX | 2001 |
| Roth, Joshua M. | USBP Laredo North, TX | 2000 |
| Rosales, Ruben | USBP Carrizo Springs, TX | 2000 |
| Rowley, Brian | USBP Colville, WA | 2001 |
| Rude, Dale A. | USBP Eureka, MT | 1993 |
| Rueda, Angel | USBP Eagle Pass, TX | 1999 |
| Russell, John | Renewable Resources, Yukon | 1994 |
| Russell, Raymond, Jr. | USBP Fort Hancock, TX | 1997 |
| Russo, Dennis M. | USBP Carrizo Springs, TX | 1997/01 |
| Rutkowski, Edmund | USBP Detroit, MI | 1994 |

| Name | Location | Year |
|---|---|---|
| Ryan, Theodore J. | USBP Del Rio, TX | 2000 |
| Ryder, Jack B. Jr. | USBP Uvalde, TX | 2001 |
| Saavedra, Raul | USBP Comstock, TX | 1997 |
| Sacasas, Magin Arsenio | USBP Eagle Pass, TX | 1999 |
| Sadler, Michael J. | USBP Oroville, WA | 1993/01 |
| Sagemuchl, Jeff | USBP Eagle Pass, TX | 1999 |
| Sagemuehl, Michael J. | USBP Eagle Pass, TX | 2001 |
| Saindon, Michael | Helena P.D., MT | 1997 |
| Salcedo, Jesse Munoz | USBP San Angelo, TX | 1998 |
| Salinas, David M. | USBP Carrizo Springs, TX | 1997/00 |
| Salinas, George | US/INS San Antonio, TX | 2003 |
| Salinas, Javier | USBP Uvalde, TX | 1998 |
| Salinas, Jose S. | USBP Carrizo Springs, TX | 2001 |
| Salinas, Juan M. | USBP Eagle Pass, TX | 2001 |
| Salinas, Martin S. | USBP Carrizo Springs, TX | 2000 |
| Salyers, Daniel | USBP Grand Forks, ND | 1994 |
| Samudio, Damon | US/INS San Antonio, TX | 2003 |
| Sanchez, Guadalupe | USBP Hebbronville, TX | 2000 |
| Sanchez, Jose | USBP Laredo North, TX | 2000 |
| Sanchez, Peter | USBP Carrizo Springs, TX | 1999/00 |
| Sanchez, Raymundo H. | USBP Alamogordo, NM | 1991 |
| Sanchez, Tino, Jr. | USBP Pembina, ND | 1994 |
| Sanderlin, James | USBP Harlingen, TX | 1993 |
| Sanders, Edward | USBP Comstock, TX | 1998 |
| Sanderson, Philip E. | Montana Dept. of Corrections, MT | 1996 |
| Sanford, Richard L. | USBP Havre, MT. | 1994 |
| Santiago, Perales | USBP Wenatchee, WA | 1993 |
| Santiago, William | USBP Eagle Pass, TX | 2001 |
| Santini, Gilbert, Jr. | USBP Eagle Pass, TX | 1997 |
| Sarabia, George | USBP Eagle Pass, TX | 1999/01 |
| Saucedo, David C. | USBP Uvalde, TX | 2001 |
| Saudeda, Marcus | USBP Brackettville, TX | 1998 |
| Sazgado, Adan | USBP Eagle Pass, TX | 1997 |
| Schaffner, Ladon R. | USBP Del Rio, TX | 2000 |
| Schifini, Tom | USBP Carrizo Springs, TX | 2000 |
| Schmerber, Tom | USBP Eagle Pass, TX | 1997 |

| | | |
|---|---|---|
| Schmidt, Nick | USBP Del Rio, TX | 1997 |
| Schweitzer, Lonny P. | USBP Grand Forks, ND | 1994 |
| Schweitzer, Michael A. | USBP Eagle Pass, TX | 1999 |
| Scott, Jeff S. | Montana Fish, Wildlife & Parks, MT | 1996 |
| Searl, James J. | USBP Del Rio, TX | 2000 |
| Seda, Julio | USBP Laredo South, TX | 2000 |
| Sepucveda, Edward | USBP Laredo North, TX | 2000 |
| Serrano, Manny | El Paso P.D., TX | 1991 |
| Serrano-Piche, Joe | USBP Eagle Pass, TX | 1999 |
| Servantes, Fernando | USBP Laredo South, TX | 2000 |
| Sexton, Marcus J. | US/INS San Antonio, TX | 2003 |
| Shafer, William | USBP Lordsburg, NM | 2003 |
| Shay, Bill T. | Grant County S/O, WA | 1993 |
| Shelton, Gary | Anaconda P.D., MT | 1996 |
| Shepard, Paul F. | FLETC Artesia, NM | 1998 |
| Sherman, James (Tim) | US Customs-Air San Angelo, TX | 1993 |
| Sherren, Frank | USBP Del Rio, TX | 2000 |
| Sherstan, Peter | RCMP Whitehorse, Yukon | 1994 |
| Shultz, Klaren D. | Grant County S/O, WA | 1993 |
| Shumaker, John D. | Olympia P.D., WA | 1993 |
| Shurley, Shea | USBP Brackettville, TX | 2000 |
| Sifuentes, Jose Jr. | USBP Carrizo Springs, TX | 1997 |
| Sifuentes, Ramon | USBP Del Rio, TX | 2000/01 |
| Siller, Agustin V. | USBP Del Rio, TX | 1997 |
| Silva, Francisco J. | USBP Eagle Pass, TX | 1997 |
| Silva, Oscar, Jr. | USBP Laredo South, TX | 2000 |
| Simmons, John R. | USBP Eagle Pass, TX | 1999 |
| Simpson, Richard (Glenn) | USBP Laredo North, TX | 2000 |
| Sinclair, Dean | USBP Uvalde, TX | 1998 |
| Sinclair, Sam J. | USBP Brackettville, TX | 2001 |
| Singer, Allan | USBP Del Rio, TX | 2000 |
| Sitton, James E. | USBP Laredo North, TX | 2000 |
| Skeroo, Austin L. II | USBP Comstock, TX | 2000 |
| Skilbred, Clifton J. | USBP Eagle Pass, TX | 1999 |
| Slater, Glen | Conservation Service B.C. | 1995 |
| Small, Stuart A. | USBP Cotulla, TX | 1992 |

| | | |
|---|---|---|
| Smalley, Darrick D. | INS Seattle, WA | 1991 |
| Smelser, Ian C. | USBP Eagle Pass, TX | 1999 |
| Smerdel, Danny O. | Cascade County S/O, MT | 1997 |
| Smith, Chekesha C. | USBP Eagle Pass, TX | 2001 |
| Smith, Cory | USBP Del Rio, TX | 2000 |
| Smith, Dave | USBP Bonners Ferry, ID | 2001 |
| Smith, Dewayne | Springfield P.D., MO | 1993 |
| Smith, Donald | US/INS San Antonio, TX | 2003 |
| Smith, Douglas | US Customs-Air San Angelo, TX | 1998 |
| Smith, Kevin | USBP Blaine, WA | 1994 |
| Smith, Mike L. | USBP Del Rio, TX | 2000 |
| Smith, Patrick J. | US Customs-Air San Angelo, TX | 1992 |
| Smith, Roderick | USBP San Angelo, TX | 1998 |
| Smith, Rosanne | USBP Del Rio, TX | 1998 |
| Sneed, Tommy C. | Burlington Northern R.R. | 1993 |
| Snyder, Mike | USBP Del Rio, TX | 1998 |
| Snyder, Timothy M. | USBP Laredo North, TX | 2000 |
| Soland, Paul L. | USBP Grand Forks, ND | 1994 |
| Soria, Luis R. | USBP Del Rio, TX | 2000 |
| Sosa, Phares A. | USBP Eagle Pass, TX | 2001 |
| Sosa, Tony R. | US/INS Eden, TX | 2003 |
| Soto, Jesus A. | USBP Laredo North, TX | 2000 |
| Soto, Jose C. | USBP Eagle Pass, TX | 1999 |
| Soto, Joseph, Jr. | US/INS San Antonio, TX | 2003 |
| Soto, Juan L. | USBP Del Rio, TX | 2000 |
| Southerland, Floyd | USBP Del Rio, TX | 1997 |
| Spangberg, Larry | Montana State Prison, MT | 1998 |
| Spence, Charles (Chip) | US Customs-Air San Angelo, TX | 1993 |
| Spratte, Albert J. | USBP Eagle Pass, TX | 2001 |
| St. Onge, Ray | Cascade County S/O, MT | 1997 |
| Stack, William P. | USBP Laredo South, TX | 2000 |
| Stafford, Steven | USBP Brackettville, TX | 1997 |
| Stahlberg, Brad | Flathead County S/O, MT | 1998 |
| Stanwick, Daniel | USBP Eagle Pass, TX | 2001 |
| Staton, Jack P. | USBP Carrizo Springs, TX | 1997 |
| Staton, Jim | Lafayette Parish S/O, LA | 1988 |

| | | |
|---|---|---|
| Steenson, Paul R. | INS Seattle, WA | 1993 |
| Stelly, Kevin P. | Lafayette Parish S/O, LA | 1991 |
| Stevens, William | USBP Del Rio, TX | 1998 |
| Steves, Richard J. | USBP Comstock, TX | 1998 |
| Stewart, Michael | USBP Cottulla, TX | 1999 |
| Stinson, James H. | USBP Wenatchee, WA | 1993 |
| Strand, Joseph C. | USBP Eagle Pass, TX | 2001 |
| Stricker, Scott V. | USBP Oroville, WA | 2001 |
| Strong, Kevin J. | USBP Havre, MT | 1994 |
| Strong, Russell | USBP Hebbronville, TX | 1999 |
| Stundal, Frank | USBP Plentywood, MT | 1994 |
| Stundal, Joseph J. | USBP Bottineau, ND | 1994 |
| Strutzel, Mike | Montana State Prison, MT | 1997 |
| Styers, Gary M. | USBP Del Rio, TX | 1998 |
| Subialdea, Gary J. | USBP Ysleta, TX | 1991 |
| Sullivan, Jonathan T. | USBP Laredo South, TX | 2000 |
| Sullivan, Tim | USBP Casa Grande, AZ | 2002 |
| Sultana, Adam | USBP Eagle Pass, TX | 1997 |
| Sumpter, David | USBP Carrizo Springs, TX | 2001 |
| Sutton, Roy G. | FLETC Artesia, NM | 1998 |
| Sweeten, Clifton, W. | USBP Eagle Pass, TX | 1999 |
| Sweeten, Randall | USBP Carrizo Springs, TX | 1997 |
| Switzer, Gergory | USBP Wenatchee, WA | 2001 |
| Sydney, Juanita | Renewable Resources, Yukon | 1994 |
| Synnott, Steven E. | USBP Laredo South, TX | 2000 |
| Tabler, Jeffrey A. | USBP Laredo South, TX | 2000 |
| Taggart, Keith | El Paso S/O, TX | 1993 |
| Talbot, Eric R. | Grant County S/O, Ephrata, WA | 2002 |
| Talley, Donald W. | US/INS San Antonio, TX | 2003 |
| Talmage, Jeffrey A. | USBP Laredo North, TX | 2000 |
| Tammen, Joe L. | USBP Fort Hancock, TX | 1991/97/03 |
| Tanniehill, Roy J. | Helena P.D., MT. | 1998 |
| Tapie, Adolfo | USBP Carrizo Springs, TX | 1997 |
| Taylor, Brian | Grant County S/O, Ephrata, WA | 2002 |
| Terlaje, Peter | USBP Del Rio, TX | 1993/97 |
| Ternes, Wayne C. | Montana Dept of Corrections, MT | 1997 |

| | | |
|---|---|---|
| Terrell, Donny R. | USBP Uvalde, TX | 2001 |
| Thibeault, Katherine | USBP Del Rio, TX | 2000 |
| Thomas, Gregory | Burlington Northern R.R. | 1993 |
| Thomas, Michael E. | USBP Del Rio, TX | 1993 |
| Thomas, Ned, Jr. | USBP Eagle Pass, TX | 1997 |
| Thompson, C.W. | FLETC Artesia, NM | 1997 |
| Thompson, Randall | USBP Las Cruces, NM | 1997 |
| Thorne, Steve | USBP Dallas, TX | 1999 |
| Thorne, Steve L. | USBP Las Cruces, NM | 1991 |
| Thorson, Travis N. | USBP Brackettville, TX | 2000 |
| Threadgill, Joe | USBP Brackettville, TX | 2000 |
| Tilsworth, Ronald W. | Burlington Northern R.R. | 1993 |
| Timmer, Kenneth L. | USBP Colville, WA. | 1993 |
| Toothman, David | USBP Eagle Pass, TX | 1997 |
| Torres, Reginald | USBP Del Rio, TX | 2000/01 |
| Torrez, Xavier | USBP Eagle Pass, TX | 2000 |
| Towner, Peter C. | USBP Del Rio, TX | 2000 |
| Townsend, Patrick G. | US Customs -Air San Angelo, TX | 1993 |
| Trevino, Cesar | USBP Carrizo Springs, TX | 2001 |
| Trevino, Jorge | US/INS Eagle Pass, TX | 2003 |
| Trevino, Jose | USBP Brackettville, TX | 1998 |
| Trevino, Sergio A. | USBP Uvalde, TX | 2000 |
| Tully, Michael W. | USBP Carrizo Springs, TX | 2001 |
| Turk, Michael P. | USBP Eagle Pass, TX | 1992 |
| Turnbull, Jim | USBP Port Angeles, WA | 1994 |
| Urban, Toney | USBP Freer, TX | 1999 |
| Urena, Jose M. | USBP Douglas, AZ | 2002 |
| Valadez, Oscar | USBP Eagle Pass, TX | 1997/00 |
| Valderrama, Luis | USBP Eagle Pass, TX | 1997 |
| Valdez, Julian | USBP Eagle Pass, TX | 2000 |
| Valdez, Nick G. | Grant County S/O, WA | 1993 |
| Valle, Andrew E. | USBP Eagle Pass, TX | 2000 |
| Van De Kop, Bryce C. | USBP Blaine, WA | 1994 |
| Vanderheyden, Wesley | USBP Lynden, WA | 1994 |
| Vandervlugt, Mark | USBP Laredo North, TX | 2000 |
| Vandiver, Joseph D. | USBP San Angelo, TX | 1998 |

| | | |
|---|---|---|
| Van Gorkom, James | USBP Del Rio, TX | 1993/97 |
| Van Haselen, Arthur | USBP Ysleta, TX | 1991 |
| Vasquez, Bernard A. | USBP Carrizo Springs, TX | 1999/2001 |
| Vasquez, Eric | USBP Del Rio, TX | 2001 |
| Vasquez, Modesto III | USBP Del Rio, TX | 2001 |
| Vasquez, Noe | US/INS San Antonio, TX | 2003 |
| Vasquez, Randall B. | USBP Laredo North, TX | 2000 |
| Vasquez, Robert | USBP Del Rio, TX | 2000 |
| Vasquez, Ross | Lafayette Parish S/O, LA | 1991 |
| Vaughan, Donald R. | FLETC Artesia, NM | 1998 |
| Vaughan, Keith | USBP Sal Angelo, TX | 1992 |
| Vega, Manuel P. | INS Seattle, WA | 1993 |
| Vega, Roberto | USBP Eagle Pass, TX | 1999/00 |
| Vela, Raul | USBP Cotulla, TX | 1993 |
| Vela, Rodolfo | USBP Laredo North, TX | 2000 |
| Velez, Robert D. | USBP Deming, NM | 1991 |
| Velquez, Bernie | USBP Las Cruces, NM | 1991 |
| Viator, Robert D. | US Customs-Air San Angelo, TX | 1993 |
| Villarreal, Hector | USBP Brackettville, TX | 1998 |
| Villarreal, Juan J. | USBP Laredo North, TX | 2000 |
| Villegas, Luis A. | USBP Hebbronville, TX | 1999 |
| Vimont, James W. | INS Yakima, WA | 1991 |
| Vinnedge, Steven | Montana Fish, Wildlife & Parks, MT | 1996 |
| Violette, Jason R.* | USBP Comstock, TX | 2000[1] |
| Volcsko, James, Jr. | USBP Eagle Pass, TX | 1999 |
| Vorobetz, Constanine | Montana State Prison, MT | 1997/98 |
| Vowell, Allen | USBP Del Rio, TX | 2000 |
| Wacker, Thomas L. | USBP Blaine, WA | 1994 |
| Wade, Bryan | USBP Laredo North, TX | 2000 |
| Wagner, Douglas M. | USBP Uvalde, TX | 1998 |
| Wainer, Don | USBP Grand Marais, MN | 1994 |
| Wakefield, Cliff | Helena P.D., MT | 1998 |
| Waldo, Richard | USBP Grand Forks, ND | 1994 |
| Walker, Clint A. | Hwy. Patrol Carrizo Springs, TX | 2000 |

* On April 6, 2000, Jason Violette, Comstock, Texas, became the 1,000th member of the Hole-in-One Club.

| | | |
|---|---|---|
| Walker, David L. | USBP Havre, MT | 1994 |
| Walker, Tommy M. | USBP Rocksprings, TX | 1998 |
| Wallace, David | USBP Eagle Pass, TX | 1997 |
| Walters, Sandy J. | USBP Carrizo Springs, TX | 1997 |
| Ward, Michael | USBP Laredo North, TX | 2000 |
| Ward, Scott R. | USBP Eagle Pass, TX | 1999/2001 |
| Warneke, William W. | Burlington Northern R.R. | 1993 |
| Warner, Kyle J. | USBP Eagle Pass, TX | 1999 |
| Warner, Michael | USBP Eagle Pass, TX | 1997 |
| Watson, Richard L. | Grant County S/O, WA | 1993/96 |
| Watts, Timothy | USBP Carrizo Springs, TX | 2001 |
| Weadon, Gregory S. | US Customs-Air San Angelo, TX | 1992 |
| Weaver, Antonio, Jr. | USBP Eagle Pass, TX | 1999 |
| Webb, Larry | USBP Comstock, TX | 1998 |
| Wehr, Ronald R. | USBP Nogales, AZ | 2002 |
| Welch, David S. | USBP Del Rio, TX | 2000 |
| Wells, Daniel N. | INS Seattle, WA | 1991 |
| Wells, Matthew E. | USBP Carrizo Springs, TX | 2000 |
| Wessner, Andrew L. | USBP Laredo North, TX | 2000 |
| West, Todd A. | US/INS San Antonio, TX | 2003 |
| Westbrook, Charles | USBP San Angelo, TX | 1992 |
| Westbrrok, Chris | USBP Nogales, AZ | 2002 |
| Westenberg, Robert | USBP Carrizo Springs, TX | 2001 |
| White, Bill | USBP Del Rio, TX | 1997 |
| Whitmore, David C. | USBP Lordsburg, NM | 2003 |
| Whitworth, Craig E. | USBP Del Rio, TX | 1997 |
| Wiles, Randall L. | USBP Laredo North, TX | 2000 |
| Wilkins, Loren P. | US Customs-Air San Angelo, TX | 1992 |
| Willcutt, Toby R. | USBP Eagle Pass, TX | 2001 |
| Willey, Kenneth | Burlington Northern R.R. | 1993 |
| Williams, Buryl L. | USBP San Angelo, TX | 1998 |
| Williams, Fred | Moses Lake, WA | 1994 |
| Williams, Jim | Burlington Northern R.R. | 1993 |
| Williams, Koby | USBP Eagle Pass, TX | 2001 |
| Williams, Paul | USBP Laredo South, TX | 2000 |
| Williams, Stephen | USBP Del Rio, TX | 1997 |

| | | |
|---|---|---|
| Wilson, Dale J. | USBP Casa Grande, AZ | 2002 |
| Wilson, Martin L. | USBP Ysleta, TX | 1992 |
| Wilson, Michael R. | USBP Blaine, WA | 1994 |
| Wilson, Robert W. | USBP Pasco, WA | 2001 |
| Winkler, Marty | USBP Ajo, AZ | 1992 |
| Winn, Edward M. | USBP Detroit, MI | 1994 |
| Winter, Randy | USBP Twin Falls, ID | 1994 |
| Wiseman, Jack | Montana Law Enforcement. Acad. Helena, MT | 1996 |
| Wishcamper, Joe | Snohomish, WA | 1996 |
| Witt, Gary D. | USBP Detroit, MI | 1994 |
| Witt, Kyle | USBP Carrizo Springs, TX | 2000 |
| Wolfe, Bradley E. | USBP Eagle Pass, TX | 1999 |
| Wolstenholme, Patrick | INS Seattle, WA | 1991 |
| Womack, William C. | USBP Willcox, AZ | 2002 |
| Woods, Richard L. | Lafayette Parish S/O, LA | 1992 |
| Woods, Thomas B. | Crime Investigation Bureau, MT | 1996 |
| Wooten, Larry L. | USBP Del Rio, TX | 2000 |
| Yarbrough, Connie | USBP Del Rio, TX | 2000 |
| Ybarra, Danny | US Customs-Air San Antonio, TX | 1993 |
| Yoakum, William P. | USBP Bakersfield, CA | 1991 |
| Yoon, Kibe | USBP Del Rio, TX | 2000 |
| Young, Kevin E. | USBP Eagle Pass, TX | 2001 |
| Young, Michael S. | USBP Eagle Pass, TX | 1997 |
| Young, Scott B. | USBP Eagle Pass, TX | 1997 |
| Zambrano, Robert | USBP Comstock, TX | 1997/00 |
| Zapata, Mariano | USBP Carrizo Springs, TX | 2000 |
| Zapata, Walter R. | USBP Uvalde, TX | 2001 |
| Zocher, George A. | USBP Grand Forks, ND | 1994 |
| Zook, Daryl | USBP Del Rio, TX | 2000 |

## Total Members of the Hole-in-One Club as of September 2004 = 1,241

Jim Gregg

## About the Author

Graduated from the University of Idaho 1956 with a BS Degree in Forestry. Began a shooting career as manager of the Seattle Gun Club in 1963. In 1969 Jim started his sightless shooting school by first teaching point shooting the shotgun for waterfowl and upland bird hunters. In 1971 Jim began a study of the psychological processes of consistency which lead to the discovery of the origin of accuracy in point-shooting the handgun. In 1974 he began holding shooting schools for the U.S. Border Patrol and has continued to train border patrol agents in almost every sector in the U.S.

# How to Order:

For more information on Jim Gregg's Shooting Schools visit:

Website: **www.JimGregg.net**

Or write:

Jim Gregg's Shooting Schools, Inc.
P.O. Box 1158
Moses Lake, Washington 98837

Email: gunguyjimgregg@yahoo.com

Softcover ISBN 0-9759068-0-1

Hardcover ISBN 0-9759068-1-X